Mrs. Kitching's Smith Island Cookbook

Mrs. Kitching's

FRANCES KITCHING

AND SUSAN STILES DOWELL

Smith Island Cookbook

SCHIFFER PUBLISHING, LTD.
4880 LOWER VALLEY ROAD,
ATGLEN, PA 19310

Published by Schiffer Publishing Ltd.

Mrs. Kitching's Smith Island Cookbook was originally published by
Tidewater Publishers in 1981

Library of Congress Cataloging-in-Publication Data

Dowell, Susan Stiles, 1949-
 Mrs. Kitching's Smith Island cookbook.

 Includes index.
1. Cookery, American—Maryland. 2. Cookery,
American—Virginia. 3. Smith Island (Md. and Va.)—
Social life and customs. I. Kitching, Frances,
1918-2003. II. Title. III. Title: Smith Island cookbook.
TX715.D746   641.59752'23   81-40043
ISBN 978-0-7643-3817-5   AACR2

ISBN: 978-0-7643-3817-5
Printed in China
6 5 4 3
First edition, 1981; tenth printing, 2011

Schiffer Books are available at special discounts for bulk purchases for sales promotions or premiums. Special editions, including personalized covers, corporate imprints, and excerpts can be created in large quantities for special needs. For more information contact the publisher:

Published by Schiffer Publishing Ltd.
4880 Lower Valley Road
Atglen, PA 19310
Phone: (610) 593-1777; Fax: (610) 593-2002
E-mail: Info@schifferbooks.com

For the largest selection of fine reference books on this and related subjects, please visit our website at:
www.schifferbooks.com
We are always looking for people to write books on new and related subjects. If you have an idea for a book please contact us at the above address.

This book may be purchased from the publisher.
Please try your bookstore first.
You may write for a free catalog.

"I would like this book in memory of my grandmother

MAGGIE W. EVANS

January 17, 1874 — April 18, 1936"

— Frances Kitching

Contents

Foreword

"Hey, gal, where you been at? We've surely missed you, that's the truth of it. But, I swagger, you ain't missed a thing!" So goes the Smith Island welcome to an off-islander whose six visits in a year to any other place on earth might elicit a friendly nod, but never unabashed pleasure. Smith Island knows no strangers. Whether you visit once or one hundred times, you will always feel right at home. Even if most of the 560 natives have noticed "the tourist from the mainland," you will never be the wiser.

Smith Island, Maryland, lies seventy-five miles directly south-east of the nation's capital, straddling the Maryland-Virginia line in the middle of the Chesapeake Bay. Four hours' driving time from Washington or Baltimore will put you at land's end in Cris-field, Maryland, within squinting distance of the four by five mile hammock. But only another thirty-five minutes by passenger ferry will land you in the heart of the finest eating grounds in the Chesapeake Bay.

Crabs, oysters, clams, fish, fowl, and game comprise the lure and major resource of this outpost ten miles off Maryland's Eastern Shore. Since 1657, Smith Islanders have been harvesting the Chesapeake Bay, and their expertise in the ways of the water is equaled only by their culinary skill in transforming its denizens to epicurean delight. Three centuries of subsisting on every species of fish and fowl known to the Bay has culminated in tried and true recipes of superior quality. Natural selection, you might say, has had a hand in producing some of the finest cooks in the region.

When your ferryboat docks in the hamlet of Ewell, you can wander the length and breadth of the island, but the best seafood in Chesapeake Bay Country cannot be found by knocking on just any door. The best seafood will be simmering in the kitchen of the most

13

renowned cook on Smith Island. Fellow tourists will be making a beeline for that kitchen, and you would be well advised to follow. For if the reputation of Frances Kitching has not prompted your pilgrimage in the first place, you have a startling and most tasty discovery ahead of you.

Mrs. Kitching's Smith Island Cookbook

Introduction

Frances Kitching will not serve muskrat or diamondback terrapin to guests in her famous Smith Island, Maryland, inn. "I do for others what I do for myself," she will tell you. "I don't like muskrat, and I don't want any little turtle fingers floating around in my soup." The golden rule is not the only unorthodox ingredient in Mrs. Kitching's cuisine. Honesty, pride, and good old-fashioned know-how have been bringing tourists to her dining room on out-of-the-way Smith Island for twenty years. Muskrat and terrapin notwithstanding, her reputation for superb victuals has made the Kitching name synonymous with the vastly appealing milieu of Chesapeake Bay cookery.

Few guests to the Kitching establishment can resist the comments column in the hotel register by the dining room door. "Fantastic—a real find!" wrote a yachtsman from Virginia. "The best meal, as good as your reputation . . ." praised a couple from Pennsylvania. "God bless your cooking." "Superlative food in the best Maryland tradition." "Quintessential." Framed letters of appreciation and four-star newspaper reviews decorate one corner of the modest room. Governors, senators, *The New York Times*, and the Smithsonian Institution's Festival of American Folklife all attest to the joys of partaking in a Frances Kitching meal. Long distance calls and letters requesting recipes have become numerous in recent years, even overwhelming, for a woman who mans the helm of her kitchen alone. "One lady called me from Virginia all in a dither because her crab loaf didn't turn out. It was the night of her dinner party! Well, whoever gave her my recipe, an' it surely wasn't me, never told her not to handle the crabmeat."

Frances Kitching professes no secrets to her success. Crab cakes plump, light, and golden without a trace of bread crumbs . . . .

17

Oyster stew, rich and creamy, swimming with gently poached oysters, great dumpling puffs, and crisp nips of sautéed onion . . . . Pie topped with meringue, homemade, hand folded, and beaded like cotton candy . . . . "That's the way it's always been done," she will tell you. Well, Mrs. Kitching, your cuisine may be a matter of course to generations of watermen's wives culling and cooking the fruits of the Chesapeake. But for legions of crab, oyster, clam, fish, fowl, and game lovers everywhere, your cuisine is an art. Your methods are still a mystery, and it is high time the world tapped that other resource of the Chesapeake Bay, the knowledge and expertise of its cooks.

CHAPTER ONE

Summer

Summertime is for seafood. And if you have any doubt about it, take a look at traffic on a July day on the Eastern Shore; triple winter's count and half the trail boards and license plates are out of state. The seafood aficionados have arrived. From the head of the Bay to its far marshy reaches, tourists are scouring the terrain for the freshest steamed crabs, the tenderest soft shell crabs, the most delectable clam fritters. "Can't blame a body for tryin'," maintains one seasoned waterman. "When you get a good meal, you don't forget it."

It was not so long ago that the best eating on the Chesapeake was out of bounds. Before 1940, visitors to isolated fishing villages had to contend with a welcome reserved for the local game warden. Today, the status of stranger has improved as tourists boat, bike, hike, and motor to every hamlet on the map, and watermen begin to accept the inevitable. "By the time the geese is leavin', the people start comin'," Captain Clarence Tyler observes. More than two hundred people a day, from the middle of June to the last of August, board Clarence's *Captain Jason* and two other ferries for the ten mile journey to Smith Island, Maryland.

What do you find on Smith Island? Besides some of the best home cooking on the Bay, it might be more appropriate to ask what will you not find on Smith Island. There are no highways, causeways, airfields, or steel span bridges marring its pancake flat twenty miles. There are no police, no jails, no mayor, no city council, and virtually no crime. Automobiles may be the most battered relics this side of a junkyard, but that is the price islanders pay for few auto mechanics, no lawsuits, and complete community harmony. "The less law," natives assert, "the more order." And they may be right, for Smith Islanders have successfully done without the world's requirements for three centuries.

21

Indoor plumbing, central heating, and electricity arrived in 1948. The telephone via the first experimental microwave radio in the country made the cultural leap in 1957. Television was established in record time, ironically enough, after the only movie theatre closed for lack of business. There are still no hospitals, supermarkets, or fast food concessions on the island, but the inhabitants will only laugh when you ask how they do without them.

The people are rugged on Smith Island; independent, big-hearted, and long on patience. Their stock derives directly from the original families named Evans, Tyler, Marshall, and Bradshaw who, legend has it, left Jamestown and St. Mary's City as dissidents in 1657. A web of consanguinity among the current population of approximately five hundred and sixty makes identity nearly impossible for the casual visitor. Even the local postmistress can confuse the four Elmer Evanses living in Ewell. Middle initials are not enough when two of the Elmers are Elmer W.

The island villages are three in number and no bigger than the tide and high ground will allow. From a distance their compact, autonomous limits emerge hazy and flat on the horizon. Only the ubiquitous church steeples distinguish the tumps from exotic outposts in the South Seas. Ewell is the undeclared capital, its mainstreet a watery thoroughfare full of workboats. Rhodes Point, formerly Rogues Point in piratical days of yore, lies a mile and a half over single lane roadway to the south. Tylerton is an island within an island, the quiet hub of hundreds of crab floats and crab shanties. Street signs in the three hamlets are confined to speed limit designations. Ten miles per hour is maximum. There are no street names. Why post them when you cannot get lost?

Acres of marsh and copse surrounding the villages are eroded from original dimensions, but they retain every bit of the lonely, pristine splendor spied by aboriginal hunting parties. Captain John Smith may have been the first white interloper when he sheltered in some nearby islands in 1608. He charted Smith Island but never named it. The Smith in question was Henry, also of Virginia, and his notoriety was inexorably established after he turned a herd of goats, or cattle, loose on one thousand acres of private land holdings.

If tourists are flocking to Smith Island in record numbers these days, local color is not the sole attraction. The lure is seafood. The lure is an inn on Smith Island. In the words of one experienced traveler: "I hate to let this one out."

Crab soup, crab cakes, clam fritters, barbecued chicken, macaroni salad, pickled carrots, corn pudding, stewed tomatoes, pineap-

22

Frances Kitching

ple casserole, green beans, yeast rolls, mama's plain cake, iced tea, and second helpings of everything complete a Frances Kitching summertime meal. For the benefit of those who have not sampled the feast, here are the recipes, compliments of Frances Kitching.

Crab Soup

1/2	pound crabmeat, regular
1	14 1/2-ounce can whole tomatoes
1	10-ounce package frozen mixed vegetables
1/2	cup diced baked ham with equal parts lean and fat
1/2	cup egg noodles (uncooked)
1/4	cup shredded cabbage
1/2	teaspoon salt
1 1/2	teaspoons Old Bay Seasoning
5	cups water

Combine all ingredients, except crabmeat, in a soup pot. Cover and cook over medium heat until vegetables are tender and noodles are cooked. Add crabmeat and simmer long enough to heat crabmeat. Serve hot. The larger the soup quantity, the better the resulting flavor will be.

Crab Cakes

1	pound crabmeat, backfin
3	tablespoons self-rising flour or pancake mix
4	shakes Worcestershire Sauce (approx. 1/8 teaspoon)
1	egg
1	tablespoon parsley flakes
1	tablespoon prepared mustard
2	generous tablespoons mayonnaise
3/4	cup vegetable oil

24

Place crabmeat in a bowl and sort through for extraneous shell. Avoid breaking the lumps. Shell encloses the lump meat; it does not perforate the nodes of flesh. Add the rest of the ingredients, except the vegetable oil, and blend together gently with a 2-pronged fork. Heat the oil in a skillet. There should be one inch of oil in the skillet. When a droplet of water spatters upon contact with the hot oil, the crab cakes can be placed in the skillet. Use an ice cream scoop to form and remove the crab cakes from the bowl. Fry a skillet full of crab cakes in the oil until golden brown on one side. Turn and fry on the other side for one minute or until golden. Remove and drain on paper towels. The same vegetable oil will cook the entire batch of crab cakes; that's several skillets full. Yield: 8 to 10 crab cakes.

Clam Fritters

12	hard clams (large cherrystone size, with their juice) or manos
1/4	teaspoon pepper
1/4	cup evaporated milk
4	tablespoons self-rising flour or pancake mix
1	egg
	peanut or corn oil for the grill

Place the clams and juice in a blender. Using a quick on-and-off method, blend clams until just minced. (They should not be pureed.) Pour minced clams into a bowl; add pepper, evaporated milk, flour, and egg and mix well. Heat the frying pan to about 375 degrees and grease lightly with oil. For each fritter, scoop out one teaspoonful of the mixture onto the hot frying pan. When just golden brown, turn with a spatula and lightly brown other side. Keep greasing frying pan as needed. Yields about 40 fritters.

Barbecued Chicken

2 1/2 - 3	pounds cut up frying chicken
1 1/4	cup ketchup
1 1/4	cup water
2	tablespoons vinegar
2	tablespoons honey
1	tablespoon prepared mustard
1	tablespoon Worcestershire Sauce
	dash chili powder

Combine ketchup, water, vinegar, honey, mustard, Worcestershire Sauce, and chili powder. Marinate the chicken in the sauce for one hour. Preheat the oven to 350 degrees. Place the chicken on a cookie sheet and be sure sauce well coats every piece of chicken. Cover the chicken with aluminum foil for the first 20 minutes. Remove the foil and bake for an additional hour. Baste during baking with remaining barbecue sauce, if desired.

Macaroni Salad

1	16-ounce package of elbow macaroni, cooked and drained
2	stalks celery, diced
1	small onion, diced
3	tablespoons green pickle relish
2	tablespoons vinegar
3	tablespoons sugar
2	tablespoons prepared mustard
1	cup mayonnaise
3	tablespoons evaporated milk

Rinse macaroni in cold water after draining to prevent sticking. Put in a large bowl and add celery, onion, and relish. Combine vinegar, sugar, mustard, mayonnaise, and evaporated milk in another bowl and blend. Pour over the macaroni and stir well with a spoon. Chill for several hours. Serves 6 to 8.

Stewed Tomatoes

1	16-ounce can whole, peeled tomatoes
1	teaspoon cinnamon
1/2	teaspoon allspice
1/8	teaspoon salt
3	tablespoons sugar
1	slice bread, crumbled
1	tablespoon butter or margarine
1	teaspoon cornstarch
2	tablespoons cold water

Place all ingredients, except butter, cornstarch, and water, in a saucepan. Cook over medium low heat for 20 minutes. Break up tomatoes with spoon. Stir occasionally. Dissolve cornstarch in water and add to saucepan. Let the mixture thicken. Remove from heat and add butter. Serve hot or cold.

Corn Pudding

1	15 1/2-ounce can cream style corn
1	13 ounce can evaporated milk
2	tablespoons cornstarch
	pinch salt
2	eggs
1	cup whole milk
	sugar to taste, about 2 tablespoons
	butter for pan, about one tablespoon

Mix the corn, evaporated milk, cornstarch, salt, eggs, and milk in a large mixing bowl and sweeten to taste with sugar. Place butter in a baking dish, $8 \times 4 \times 1$ 1/2 inches. Spread the butter thickly so that it will rise to the top during baking. Pour in the corn mixture and place the pan in an oven preheated to 350 degrees. Bake for 45 minutes or until firm when the pan is shaken.

Pickled Carrots

2	pounds cooked carrots, thinly sliced
1	cup creamy French dressing, commercial or homemade
1	10 3/4-ounce can tomato soup
1	teaspoon each: salt, dry mustard, and paprika
1	cup vinegar
1	cup brown sugar
2	medium onions, thinly sliced

Combine and blend well: French dressing, soup, salt, mustard, paprika, vinegar, and brown sugar. Immerse the carrots in the marinade and chill in the refrigerator for one hour. Top with sliced onions and serve. A large portion will keep in the refrigerator for 2 weeks.

Pineapple Casserole

2	cups crushed pineapple (do not drain)
1/3	cup sugar
3	cups fresh bread crumbs
2	eggs
2	slices white bread, crusts removed
1/4	cup butter or margarine
	butter for baking dish, about one tablespoon

Combine pineapple, sugar, and bread crumbs. Mix with a spoon to a uniform consistency. Add the 2 slightly beaten eggs and mix again with a spoon. Grease a 1 1/2-quart shallow baking dish with one tablespoon of butter and spread the pineapple mixture evenly in the dish. Cube the 2 slices of white bread and distribute the dabs evenly atop the pineapple mixture. Melt the 1/4 cup of butter in a small saucepan and spoon over each bread cube. Bake at 350 degrees for one hour. Serves 6 easily.

Green Beans

2	pounds fresh green beans, snapped, strings removed
2	quarts water
1/4	pound salt pork

Cut up the salt pork in slices, semiattached to the salty rind. Put in a pot with the 2 quarts of water. Heat and add the beans to the water. Cook until the beans are tender. Remove the salt pork and serve. You may serve the salt pork. Some people like it.

28

Yeast Rolls

2 1/2	cups flour
1	package dry yeast
1/2	cup lukewarm water
4 1/2	tablespoons sugar
3/4	teaspoon salt
1/4	cup softened butter
1	egg
3	tablespoons vegetable oil

Dissolve yeast in 1/2 cup warm water and set aside. In a large bowl, sift together the flour, salt, and sugar. Add the butter, slightly beaten egg and vegetable oil to the sifted flour mixture. Mix with a wooden spoon or hands until uniformly blended. Slowly add the yeast dissolved in water and blend until a dough is formed. The dough must be moist so add more water 1/4 cup at a time until dough is sticky. Knead for 5 minutes. Set aside in a bowl in a warm place and cover with a cloth for one hour. Knead once more for 5 minutes. Form rolls and place on cookie sheet. Before baking, let the rolls rise until doubled. Preheat oven to 350 degrees. Bake rolls for 20 minutes at 350 degrees. Turn the temperature down to 275 degrees for 5 minutes and remove.

Mama's Plain Cake

1	cup butter or margarine
2	tablespoons vegetable shortening
5	eggs
3	cups sugar
3	cups flour
1/4	teaspoon salt
3/4	cup evaporated milk
1/4	cup water
2	teaspoons lemon, walnut, or butternut flavoring, optional

Cream butter and sugar. Add eggs. Sift together flour and salt and add to batter. Slowly add milk and water. Beat until creamy. Add flavoring, if desired. Grease a 10-inch tube pan, then dust with flour. Turn out excess flour, and pour batter into pan. Bake for one hour and 45 minutes at 350 degrees. Top with fresh fruit in season.

Smith Islanders do not tell fish stories. There are too many experts in the neighborhood to examine the evidence. So when crab potter Eddie Evans tells you he caught a one and three quarter pound blue crab with a twenty-eight-inch claw span not three miles from Smith Island, believe him, or you may find yourself staring into the beady, stalked eyes of the biggest blue crab you ever saw, mounted on Eddie's den wall. Any further skepticism will be dowsed with Eddie's famous shark story, the best rendition of which can be had at the local general store.

> Eddie boy'd keep seein' his fin everyday, goin' after the fish he'd dump from his crab pots. Eddie was tellin' it around there's sharks in the area. Fishin' fellas there in Crisfield said, "Aw, those boys weren't seein' no sharks. They're seein' stingrays. You know, those little fins bobbin' in the air. Lotta watermen think stingrays are sharks." Ole Eddie got to thinkin' about that and got wonderin' if he could catch the thing. He got a hook with a handle on it, and he tied some rope to it with an empty five-gallon oil drum at the other end to use for a buoy. He tried for two or three days to hook that shark but he didn't get close enough. One day he did. The shark come right up to the boat and opened his mouth. Eddie shot that hook into his mouth, caught him, turned him loose, throwed the can overboard and that shark kept goin' round and round. The pressure of the can on top the water eventually wore him down. It took six guys hauling on that line one hour to get him in. Eddie hung him up to his wharf. "Told those fishin' fellas over t'Crisfield" he'd caught a stingray and "to come on over an' see it."

Eight foot, four hundred-pound sharks and mammoth male Atlantic blue crabs are not in a normal day's work for a Smith Island crab potter, nor are bustin' seas and waterspouts "twistin' like an eggbeater and big enough to swamp a boat," but woe to the waterman who doesn't expect them, at any time. The work does not get monotonous, only harder as the grueling business wears on through the summer, of gaffing, heaving, culling, rebaiting, and returning some two hundred wire mesh crab pots each weighing twenty pounds when wet and full. The exercise takes seven hours, averaging one pot every two minutes. A full day, however, goes ten hours or longer, beginning at 3:30 A.M. and ending by midafternoon when the catch has been delivered to the mainland Eastern Shore market.

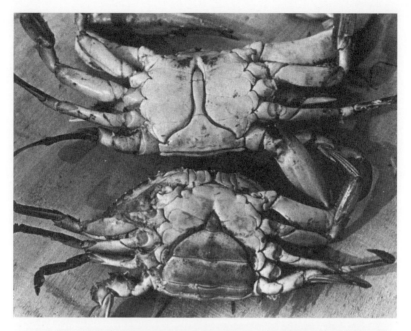

Top. A Jimmy (mature male) crab above, and a sook (mature female). *Bottom.* A crab that has just moulted—a soft shell crab.

Most Smith Island crab potters utilize the license from May until September each year. A few die-hards like Eddie Evans will go the limits of the season, April 1 through December 31. Only when there is nary a crab to be caught in the Chesapeake Bay will Eddie turn his mind to oystering. "That snow does something that nothing does. No matter when it comes, it cuts crabbing off. I guess that's the signal for them to go snug up."

One crab pot has been known to trap anywhere from zero to fifty crabs at one time and anything from a seething mass of stinging sea nettles to one thrashing monster of a fifty-pound rockfish. No one goes looking to pot rockfish. There is frequently a fine attached to such accidents. On the other hand, you do not ignore the tasty godsend. Eddie Evans dragged the fused mass of fish and pot home, extracted the behemoth with wire cutters, weighed him, photographed him, and ate him. "And if I didn't have proof," says Eddie, "I wouldn't be tellin' it."

The Atlantic blue crab that ventures into crab pots after fish bait comes in all shapes, sizes, and stages of development, nearly every one of them delicious. True to its Latin species name, *Callinectes sapidus* is, indeed, savory. Crab potters will keep almost all forms of the blue crab that are marketable, but their primary target is the hard crab, or crab with a hard shell.

"Jimmy" crabs, or males, are the fattest and meatiest form of the hard shell blue crab. Mrs. Kitching advises that you use nothing but the biggest, freshest jimmies for a steamed hard crab feast. You can identify jimmies in the seafood marketplace by looking on the underside of the shell. The male's abdominal apron will be shaped like an inverted T. Avoid steaming "sooks," or mature females, identified by an abdominal apron in the shape of a half circle crowned with a small V. Sooks, unless pregnant, do not contain the quantity of meat that jimmies do. Pregnant sooks, or "sponges," may be astoundingly plump and piquantly peppered with eggs, but you will not find Smith Islanders selling or eating the meat. Being Marylanders and fishing in Maryland waters, Smith Island watermen are prohibited by law from marketing them, unlike their neighbors five miles to the south in Virginia.

Fresh steamed crabmeat, already picked and packaged, derives from jimmies and sooks. Mrs. Kitching favors lump crabmeat, or backfin as it is commercially called. She advises that you sort gently through the crabmeat for any pieces of shell that pickers might have overlooked. "If you don't, your guest will, but he'll be doing his picking at the dinner table."

When working with crabmeat, always take great care not to pull apart the lumps of meat, and when combining your ingre-

32

dients, use a fork. Never break apart or mash the crabmeat. Use an ice cream scoop to form exceptionally large and rounded mounds for Maryland crab cakes. Crabmeat requires a minimum of seasoning. Mrs. Kitching describes the meat as sweet and needing very little enhancement. Frozen crabmeat, on the other hand, will need the extra kick lost through freezing. To defrost crabmeat, allow cold water to run through the meat placed in a colander. When defrosted completely, let the meat drip dry. Combine the crabmeat with your ingredients when the meat is no longer dripping.

HARD CRAB RECIPES

Crab Balls

1	pound crabmeat, special
3	tablespoons self-rising flour
1	egg
3	drops hot pepper sauce
1	tablespoon prepared mustard
2	tablespoons mayonnaise
1	tablespoon Old Bay Seasoning

Put crabmeat in a bowl, and gently sort through it for pieces of shell with 2-pronged fork. Remove shell. Add all ingredients, and mix gently until thoroughly blended. Form into balls. Deep fry until golden. Yields about 30 balls.

Crab Creole

1	pound crabmeat, preferably backfin
1	10 3/4-ounce can tomato soup
1	envelope Spatini Spaghetti Sauce
1/2	diced green pepper
1	medium onion, diced
1 1/4	cups white rice

Boil white rice according to directions and set aside. In a large skillet combine Spatini, tomato soup, pepper, onion, and one tomato soup can full of water. Simmer. Add the crabmeat to the tomato sauce and when piping hot, pour over rice and serve.

33

Crab Hors d'Oeuvre

1/2	pound crabmeat, preferably backfin
1	8-ounce package cream cheese
1	tablespoon whole milk
1	tablespoon minced onion
1/2	teaspoon horseradish
1	3-ounce package slivered almonds
	salt and pepper to taste

Combine crabmeat, cream cheese, whole milk, minced onion, horse-radish, salt, and pepper in a mixing bowl with a fork, taking care not to break lumps of crabmeat while blending. Having the cream cheese at room temperature will facilitate the blending. Transfer the mixture to a one-quart shallow baking dish. Do not pack. Sprinkle the top with slivered almonds. Bake at 350 degrees for 20 minutes, or until lightly brown on top. Cut up into small squares. Let sit for twenty minutes until firm, then serve.

Crabmeat Salad

1	pound crabmeat, backfin or special
1	cup finely diced celery
1/2	teaspoon salt
1/4	teaspoon white pepper
4	shakes of Worcestershire Sauce (approx. 1/8 teaspoon)
1	teaspoon lemon juice
1/2	cup mayonnaise
5	teaspoons creamy French or thousand island salad dressing, optional
8	medium sized tomatoes
	lettuce

Put crabmeat in a bowl, and gently sort through it for shell with a 2-pronged fork. Remove bits of shell. Add diced celery, salt, pepper, Worcestershire Sauce, lemon juice, mayonnaise, and salad dressing, mixing gently with the 2-pronged fork. When uniformly blended, put into refrigerator and chill for one hour. Decoratively slash each tomato nearly to the base in six sections, discarding the top and some of the inside. Fill each tomato with crabmeat mixture, and serve on a bed of lettuce.

Quick Crabmeat Salad

1   pound crabmeat, backfin or special
1/2   cup mayonnaise
1/4   cup green pickle relish
4   shakes Worcestershire Sauce (approx. 1/8 teaspoon)
       dash white pepper
8   medium sized tomatoes
       lettuce

Combine crabmeat, mayonnaise, relish, Worcestershire Sauce and white pepper in manner prescribed for previous crabmeat salad. Chill for one hour. Fill decoratively cut tomatoes with crabmeat mixture and serve on a bed of lettuce.

French Fried Jimmy Crabs

1   dozen medium sized male crabs, washed and scrubbed in water, with legs, back shells, and innards removed
1   pound crabmeat, regular
1   scant cup flour
1   scant cup milk
1   teaspoon salt
1   teaspoon celery seed
2   teaspoons parsley
1   egg
1   teaspoon Old Bay Seasoning
1   tablespoon vegetable oil
       enough vegetable oil for deep frying

Combine all ingredients, except crab, crabmeat, and vegetable oil, to make a batter. Stir one tablespoon of vegetable oil into the batter. Fill crab crevices, where innards were removed, with crabmeat and press the crabmeat firmly into the crevice to secure. Holding each stuffed crab with tongs, dip into batter, then place in the deep fry filled with very hot vegetable oil. Completely cover the crab and fry individually for seven minutes or until golden.

Crab Burgers

1	pound crabmeat, backfin or special
1/2	small onion, finely diced
1/4	green pepper, finely diced
1	tablespoon mayonnaise
	dash Old Bay Seasoning
8	hamburger rolls
8	slices mozzarella cheese

Cut hamburger rolls in half. Butter each half and toast lightly in broiler. In a bowl combine crabmeat, onion, pepper, mayonnaise, and Old Bay Seasoning. Cover each of 8 hamburger rolls thickly with crabmeat mixture, and top with a slice of cheese. Place 8 burgers on cookie sheet and bake in a 350-degree oven until crabmeat is heated, and cheese is melted. Remove from oven, top with other half of hamburger roll, and serve.

Crab Loaf

2	pounds crabmeat, backfin or special
1	small onion, finely diced
1/2	medium green pepper, finely diced
3	tablespoons butter or margarine
1	cup milk
3	teaspoons cornstarch
2	eggs
3	tablespoons mayonnaise
1	tablespoon prepared mustard
2	teaspoons Old Bay Seasoning (use one teaspoon for less spicy crabmeat)
1/4	cup butter or margarine
8	slices of bread without crusts, cubed

Sauté onion and pepper in 3 tablespoons of butter or margarine. Dissolve cornstarch in one cup of milk and add to sautéed onion and pepper. Stir over low heat until a smooth paste results. Set aside. Put crabmeat in bowl, and pick through for extraneous shell. Add the eggs which have been slightly beaten beforehand. Add the mayonnaise, mustard, Old Bay Seasoning, 4 slices of the cubed bread, and the cornstarch mixture to the crabmeat, and stir gently. Spoon the mixture into a 10 × 14-inch baking dish and spread evenly. Do not pack. Place the remaining bread cubes on top of the crabmeat mixture. Melt 1/4 cup of butter or margarine, and spoon over bread cubes. Bake at 350 degrees for 35 minutes. Cut into 3-inch squares, and serve on a platter garnished with cherry tomatoes.

Crab Imperial

1	pound crabmeat, preferably backfin
1	medium sized green pepper, finely diced
2	tablespoons butter or margarine
1/4	cup whole milk
1	teaspoon flour
1	teaspoon Old Bay Seasoning
1	teaspoon prepared mustard
1	tablespoon mayonnaise
8	crab carapaces (either pyrex ones or the real thing, washed well)
1	egg
3	tablespoons mayonnaise
	paprika

Sauté diced pepper in 2 tablespoons of butter or margarine. Dissolve the flour in the milk and add it to the sautéed pepper. Stir over low heat until a smooth paste results. Put the crabmeat in a bowl, and gently sort through for extraneous bits of shell. Add the Old Bay Seasoning, mustard, mayonnaise, and green pepper/white sauce to the crab-meat. Blend the ingredients gently with a 2-pronged fork so as not to break crabmeat lumps. Use an ice cream scoop to fill crab carapaces with crabmeat mixture. In a separate bowl, beat one egg. Add 3 tablespoons of mayonnaise and beat until well blended. Spoon the mixture atop each crabmeat-filled shell. Top with a good dusting of paprika for each crab shell. Bake at 350 degrees for 15 minutes, or until brown.

Steamed Crabs

12-16	alive and kicking male crabs, the larger, the better, well washed with garden hose
2	cups vinegar
1	cup water
1	teaspoon salt
3-4	tablespoons Old Bay Seasoning

Pour vinegar and water into a large 12-quart steamer. Add salt, Old Bay Seasoning, and crabs to the steamer and cook for 35 minutes. Serve hot. Follow pictures below for how to pick the meat from steamed crabs.

Stewed Jimmy Crabs

12-15	medium sized live male crabs with back shells and loose innards (including attached gills) removed
1	quart tap water
4	strips bacon
2	tablespoons flour
1	teaspoon salt
1/2	teaspoon pepper
1	medium sized onion, diced
6-8	medium sized potatoes, washed and peeled

Remove all traces of mud from the crabs. Pull off the back shell and innards. Set a 10-quart pot on the burner. Lay 4 strips of bacon on the bottom of the pan and fry. Set aside bacon. To the bacon grease add 2 tablespoons of flour. Brown the flour in the grease, then add one quart of water to the pot. Add the diced onion, the cleaned crabs, and the salt and pepper. Cook over medium heat for 25 minutes, then add potatoes. When potatoes are cooked through, remove the stew from the heat and serve hot. For hearty crab eaters, allow 4 crabs per serving. This is a traditional waterman's meal, relished for its flavor and the respite it affords wives from picking crabmeat. The eater, you see, does his own crabmeat picking. There is no etiquette, by the way, to the eating. Just dig in.

39

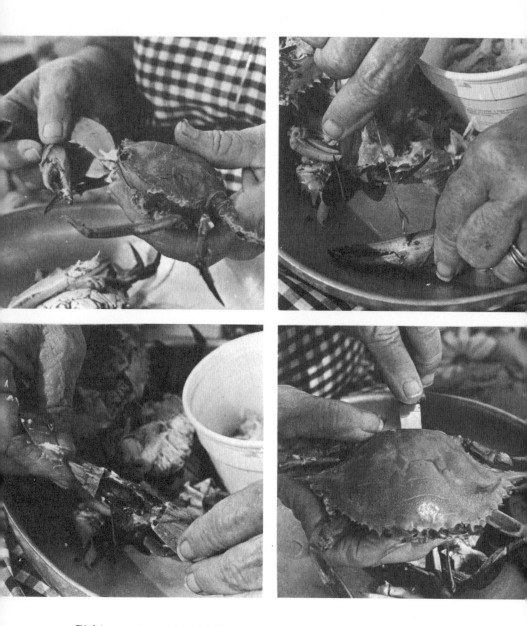

Picking a steamed crab: *Top.* Pull off the claws. To remove claw meat, puncture the inside hard shell with knife just below pinchers. *Bottom.* Break the shell and pull. The claw meat will come out intact, attached to the pincher end of the claw. Remove the top shell by sliding knife just under back end of shell.

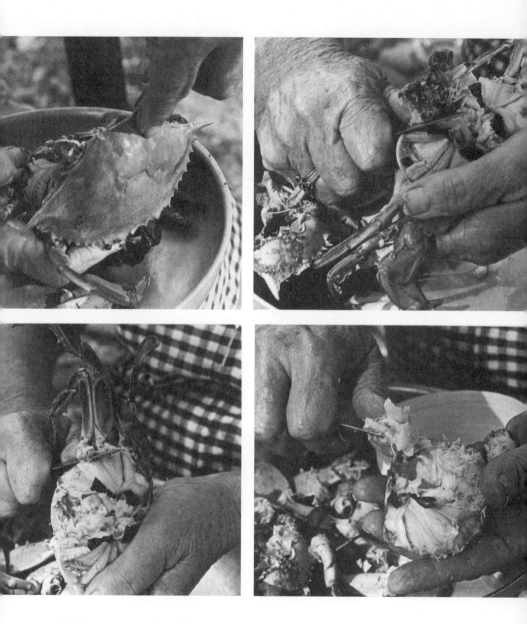

Picking a steamed crab: (cont'd.) *Top.* Pry the shell off the crab and discard. Cut off eye region with knife. *Bottom.* Cut away walking and swimming legs, scrape out soft matter running through middle of crab, and cut away the fibrous gills overlaying the hard body section. With knife or fingers, pick the meat from each chamber in the crab's body.

41

Stewed Crabmeat and Dumplings

1	pound crabmeat, special
4	slices of salt pork or bacon
2	medium potatoes, diced
1	medium onion, diced
1/4	teaspoon salt
	dash black pepper
2	cups water
10	dumplings

Fry the salt pork in the bottom of a 4-quart pot. Remove the pork, leaving the grease on the bottom of the pot. Add the potatoes, onion, salt, pepper, and 2 cups of water to the pot and cook over medium heat for 5 minutes. Add the crabmeat atop the vegetables. Do not stir. Bring to a boil. Make 10 small, circular pancakes, about 3 inches in diameter, from dumpling dough (recipe to follow), and drop them one at a time into the boiling crab stew. Reduce the heat to simmer and cook for 15 minutes, or until the dumplings are no longer doughy. Serve with a tossed salad.

Dumplings

1	cup flour
3/4	teaspoon salt
1	teaspoon baking powder
1/4 - 1/3	cup water

Sift flour, salt, and baking powder. Add water slowly and knead to form a dough. Sprinkle flour on waxed paper, and roll out dough to 1/4-inch thickness. Cut out dumplings with a knife or cookie cutter in the shape and size desired, and cook as directed.

Crabmeat-Shrimp au Gratin

1/2	pound crabmeat, special
2	pounds shrimp, steamed, shelled and deveined
2	tablespoons butter
2	tablespoons flour
1	cup milk
1	teaspoon prepared mustard
1	teaspoon hot pepper sauce
1	teaspoon Worcestershire Sauce
2	tablespoons dry sherry
1	teaspoon onion flakes
1	teaspoon parsley flakes
	salt and pepper to taste
1	cup medium sharp cheese, grated

Melt butter over low flame. Add flour to form a paste. Slowly stir in milk to make white sauce. Combine remaining ingredients, except cheese, shrimp, and crabmeat, and add to white sauce. Fold in shrimp and crabmeat. Pour into a casserole dish, top with cheese, and bake at 350 degrees for 25 minutes.

SOFT SHELL CRABS

"I couldn't eat soft crabs over to them mainland restaurants. 'Tried to once, but they was too juicy for me." Smith Islanders are of one mind when it comes to the preparation and delectation of their number one resource and favorite food. Crab scraping watermen would sooner fix their own than sit down to a prefrozen, deep fried "jumbo" of the restaurant trade. "Clean it out good, and fry it slow" is the culinary maxim of five hundred and sixty-odd soft shell crab fancying natives. Not even gourmets in New York, Paris, San Francisco, or London who have waited all winter for their first bite of the delicacy can compete with the persnickety palates on Smith Island.

As the undisputed champion producers of soft shell crabs on the Chesapeake Bay, Smith Islanders are spoiled. What you pay $6 to $20 a dozen for at the local seafood market, Smith Islanders eat for free every May through September. The volume of business is prodigious for such a small place. Harvested soft crabs outnumber

the natives by as much as 200 to 1 in peak season. The production is even more impressive when you realize that the Chesapeake Bay, with Smith Island in the lead, feeds the nation ninety-five percent of its total soft shell crab intake.

So why, in the midst of summertime when the crabbing season is at its height, are the island lanes deserted and the houses still except for the omnipresent drone of air conditioners? Scrub pine, fig, and pomegranate trees are inert in the heat. Even the "thurfur," the island's access waterway, is placidly free of work-boat activity. This idyll belies a frenetic industriousness unapparent to the visitor's eye. Beneath the surface of the waters surrounding Smith Island that appear so calm are hundreds of thousands of Atlantic blue crabs intent on the business of shedding their shells. Doggedly pursuing them are virtually all the island's male population from six to sixty, plying the creeks, coves, and guts with an ingenious net device called the "crab scrape." Whoever remains back home operates the family crab shanties, overseeing the moulting process of thousands of impounded crabs.

The blue crab may shed its chitinous shell as many as twenty-three times in its natural three-year lifespan in order to accommodate the growth of its soft inner body. Crab scrapes will comb the grassy shallows all summer routing out the "peelers" to bring back to the shanty floats where they are carefully tended until moulting is accomplished. Greens, white signs, pink signs, red signs, ranks, busters, softs, buckrams, and doublers: the crab moulting terminology can make your head spin. Every waterman, and woman, grows up reading the subtle signs preparatory to moulting. Some are easy. Doublers are the piggyback riders in the precopulating position. "You can get a sex lesson from those crabs," watermen tell you, with no blushes as they initiate the explanation. Some signs would take a novice years to identify. The white sign refers to a faint rim of white on the crab's swimming leg, indicating the moult to be two weeks hence. Learning it is about as easy as learning the names and locations of every spit and gut within twenty miles of Smith Island, which, by the way, watermen know as well.

And if culling the soft crabs is not enough, there is the sorting and packing of the final product which must be caught in a soft shell state before six hours elapse when the shell grows hard again. Mediums, hotels, primes, jumbos, and whales are the size categories. The working hours could demoralize an ordinary man: 3:30 A.M. to 3:00 P.M. at peak season in the steamy, buggy tidal marshes. Only the actual physical labor of hauling two fully laden

100-pound scrapes every fifteen minutes makes you wonder about the mortality rate among watermen. One crab scraping waterman pulled up an oil burner in his scrape. "It was hotter 'n fire that day," said a waterman working the same cove. "An he was carryin' that stove on his bow to keep from pullin' it up somewhere else. 'It's chilly a bit, this mornin',' I yelled to him, 'But not cold enough to put a stove aboard.'"

Part of the delight in eating a soft shell crab is being able to eat the whole thing, but Mrs. Kitching advises that you remove a bit of extra baggage first. The top "shed" or shell is unnecessary as are the loose innards. Cut off the mouth and the stalked eyes. Cut out, as well, the gills beneath the shell and the two round white posterior appendages. Though everything is edible, Mrs. Kitching touts a more savory, less juicy mouthful with the extras removed. Buy the prime sized soft shell crabs that run four-and-one-half to five inches across the top shell. They are perfect for single servings in your seafood banquet. The best sautéed soft crabs will be fresh, but if you buy them frozen or freeze your own, just defrost as you would any other meat. In the sautéing process you might experiment with a variety of spices sprinkled sparingly atop the flour dredged surface, among them Old Bay Seasoning, parsley, and paprika. Always remember, however, a little bit of spice goes a long way on crabmeat.

SOFT SHELL CRAB RECIPES

Sautéed Soft Shell Crab #1

4	soft shell crabs, preferably of "prime" size
1/2	cup flour
1/4	teaspoon salt
1/8	teaspoon black pepper
4	tablespoons vegetable oil

Combine flour, salt, and pepper in a bowl. Dredge each crab thoroughly in the seasoned flour. Heat the vegetable oil in a skillet until a droplet of water spatters upon contact with the hot oil. Place each of the flour coated soft shell crabs in the skillet. Cover and fry on both sides until golden. Serve hot.

Sautéed Soft Shell Crab #2

4	soft shell crabs, preferably of "prime" size
1/2	cup pancake mix
4	tablespoons vegetable oil

Dredge each crab thoroughly in the pancake mix. Heat the vegetable oil in a skillet until a droplet of water spatters upon contact with the hot oil. Place each crab in the skillet. Cover and fry on both sides until golden. Serve hot.

Deep Fried Buckrams

12	buckrams, preferably of "medium" size (3 1/2 inches across the shell)
1	cup flour
1	teaspoon salt
1	egg
1/8	teaspoon Worcestershire Sauce
1	teaspoon celery seed
1	cup whole milk
1	tablespoon parsley flakes
1	cup vegetable oil

Buckrams are soft shell crabs with shells hardened to a paper, crinkly hard, thickness. The islanders procure the delicacy easily enough, but for those beyond the Tidewater region, accessibility is a problem. Inquire at your local seafood market for a special order.

Combine flour, salt, egg, Worcestershire Sauce, celery seed, milk, and parsley flakes in a bowl. Blend well. Heat the vegetable oil in a skillet. When hot, take one tablespoon of the oil from the skillet and add it to the flour batter. Mix it in. Dip each of the 12 buckrams into the batter and then place into the hot oil. Fry on each side until golden brown. Serve hot.

CLAMS

When you say "clam" to a Smith Islander, explain yourself. Do you mean "clam" or "mano?" To a waterman living south of Kedges Strait a clam is a mollusk with a hard shell, an established delicacy marketed according to size as cherrystones or chowder clams, and

48

indigenous to the higher salinity levels of the lower Bay. Everywhere else on the Chesapeake, a clam is a mollusk with a soft shell, a newcomer to the Bay seafood scene and the very same delight served steamed or fried in New England. To clarify the confusion, use waterman's lingo. Call the hard shell variety "hard clams." Call the soft shell clams "manos" or "maninose clams." No one knows where the name maninose came from. It sounds Indian, and that is its probable origin.

Of the two clam varieties, manos are the more abundant and the more ignored in Bay country. Their culinary qualities are peerless, however, as New Englanders well know and wisely keep mum about, since they import most of their supply from the Chesapeake Bay. Before 1951, a mano was only considered fit for the hook end of a fishing rod. "Clam snouts" advertising at roadside bait stands gave the creature an immunity from consumption which most Bay species must become almost extinct to enjoy. Even watermen held the species in contempt when, after 1951, an innovative clam dredging contraption catapulted clam yields and at the same time left a trail of buried oysters in its wake. What is merely raked out of mud flats at low tide in New England is concealed in the Chesapeake Bay under a foot of mud and ten to twenty feet of water. The donnybrook over manos has been resolved now, thanks to studies at the University of Maryland's Chesapeake Biological Laboratory. Manos are designated in some beds, oysters in others. The designation does not keep the two varieties of mollusks apart, just the fishermen. Mano clammers and oystermen by law must keep their distance. Faint snickers from the oystering contingent, however, may still accompany the sight of a mano boat broiling up the foam in its lurching reach to starboard.

One of approximately four hundred soft shell clammers in the state of Maryland lives on Smith Island. There used to be sixteen on the island, but watermen, independent as they are, "like a change of jobs." Fifteen have returned to the traditional occupations of oystering and crabbing. Dickie Evans has been mano dredging for four years now, and he is not going to change. "I go after manos. They have a bigger market and wider fishing area than (hard) clams. (Hard) clams, you just scoop off the bottom with a different rig. There's a fella over t'Crisfield does the (hard) clamming." Dickie is allowed fifteen bushels a day by law, year round. In the summertime he must be off the water by 1 P.M. to insure the clams stay fresh and bacteria free. Four days is the average work week, not by choice but by weather conditions. Winds stronger than fifteen miles per hour and seas higher than one-and-one-half feet will pull the boat's hydro-escalator conveyor

49

belt off the bottom where it must lodge to extract the buried manos. Still, the work is profitable and, by Dickie Evans's accounting, satisfying as well. He offers palatable proof in two simple mano recipes of his own:

"Cantaloupes": Find yourself the biggest manos you can. We get them six inches across. We call them cantaloupes. Cut the bodies in fourths. Cut the snouts in little pieces. Dredge all the parts in flour seasoned with salt and pepper. Fry in a little vegetable shortening until cooked through.

Steamed Manos: Take two or three dozen manos, rinsed of mud. Put in a steamer pot with one cup of boiling water or vinegar on the bottom. Dowse the clams generously with Old Bay Seasoning and top with a stalk of celery. Cover and steam for fifteen minutes or until the shells open. Serve with melted butter, or a cocktail sauce of one-half cup ketchup, enough vinegar to thin ketchup, one-half teaspoon of Old Bay Seasoning, and a little black pepper.

CLAM RECIPES

Clam Pie

2	9 inch pie crusts for top and bottom of pie
8-10	chowder (hard) clams
3/4	cup milk
2	eggs, well beaten
1/2	cup soda cracker crumbs
1	teaspoon salt
1/4	teaspoon pepper
2	tablespoons butter

Prepare pie crust, setting aside top crust. In mixing bowl, combine clams, milk, eggs, cracker crumbs, salt, and pepper. Pour into pie shell and dot with pieces of butter. Cover with top crust, trimming overhanging pastry to 1/2 inch. Fold it under and flute to insure no leaking. Cut several one-inch slits near center of pie. Place in 450-degree oven for 15 minutes, then reduce heat and bake at 350 degrees for 30 minutes.

Baked Hard Clams

1   dozen cherrystone (hard) clams
     crackers
     vinegar sauce or ketchup sauce

Wash clams in several waters and place on a cookie sheet. Preheat oven to 350 degrees. Put clams in the oven for 8 to 10 minutes, or until shells just open. Remove from the oven and cut the muscle of each clam connecting the body with the top shell. Discard top shell. Also sever the muscle connecting the body with the bottom shell, for easy eating. Serve with vinegar seasoned with salt and pepper, or ketchup seasoned with salt and hot pepper sauce.

Clam Chowder

2   dozen chowder (hard) clams
2   large onions
2   cups water
4   large potatoes
1   quart whole milk
1   tablespoon butter
     salt and pepper to taste

Before using any clams, discard those which do not close their shells immediately upon being handled. The night before preparing the chowder, wash the clams in several waters, then place them in a plastic bag. Put the bag(s) of clams in the freezer overnight. Next morning, take the clams from the freezer and set in the sink. Allow 1/2 hour for clams to open their shells. Hasten the process by running cold water over the clams. The overnight freezing will facilitate prying open the shells. When the shells are open, slip a paring knife inside and cut the muscles. Shuck the clams and discard the shells. Chop up the clams finely and save the juice in the process. Dice the onions and add them to the clams. In a large saucepan, add enough water to boil the potatoes. When cooked, remove the potatoes and mash thoroughly. Add the mashed potatoes to the clams. Heat the quart of milk just short of boiling and add to the clams, onion and potatoes. Pour it all into a soup pot and simmer. Add salt and pepper to taste and one table-spoon of butter. Serve piping hot.

Clam Puffs

15	cherrystone (hard) clams
1	tablespoon parsley flakes
1	teaspoon minced garlic, optional
2	drops hot pepper sauce
2/3	cup instant mashed potatoes
2	cups seasoned dry bread crumbs
2	cups peanut or corn oil

Place shucked clams and juice in a blender. Blend clams in an on-and-off technique until just minced. Pour into a bowl and add parsley, garlic, hot pepper sauce, potatoes, and bread crumbs. Mix together with a spoon, then form tablespoon-sized balls. Drop into 2 cups of oil and deep fry until golden puffs form.

CHAPTER TWO

Fall

The Chesapeake turns steely blue in the fall. Cold gusts chase the sunlight off the water and usher in legions of migrating waterfowl. The watermen of summer register every nuance. One by one, they relinquish crabbing for the oystering, fishing, and hunting of fall.

Every man has his preference. Wat Kitching heads his boat down to the Outer Banks for a week of commercial fishing. Lowry Evans is oystering promptly on the first day of the season. If the weather holds, Dallas Bradshaw may be fishing his peeler floats until October. Only Alan Smith gets to go gunning full time during the duck hunting season. Many a waterman is itching to get those geese in his gun sights, but few can afford the indulgence. " 'Ain't not much gunnin' goes on 'round here no more," they concur. "People got out of it. 'Lot of 'em got caught [breaking the law]. 'Cain't afford to get caught no more 'cause our boats and outboards get taken away."

Alan Smith is the exception. He manages a gun club on the island. When he takes on a hunting party, he has the group in a duck blind from 7 A.M. to 4 P.M. The nine-hour wait can be barren. By Smith's reckoning, ducks are smart. Once shot at, they avoid the blinds. Inclement weather and low tide will raft them up in the shallows, but hunting parties are seldom able to take advantage of the island's rough weather. Even the natives wisely refuse to cross Tangier Sound in choppy seas. A few watermen, discouraged from oystering by wind and snow, will brave the marshes for a good kill. Some never return. "One chance run out on you, you've had it," says Alan Smith, Jr. "If you're out in a snow blizzard 'n your outboard breaks down, that's it."

Strict enforcement of gunning laws has turned many died-in-the-wool hunters to other pursuits. A fair number have cashed in

54

on decoy carving. Robely Bradshaw professes so many back orders that he has lost count. "If I did this to make a livin', I'd starve to death," he laughs. "It takes too long!" A handful of Smith Islanders collect arrowheads in their spare time. Someone recently estimated that there are close to ten thousand Indian artifacts squirreled away in homes on the island.

Alan Smith, who spends at least as much time arrowhead hunting as he does gunning, once found 126 arrowheads in one day on the beaches fringing Smith Island. When Smith was a boy, he made bets with friends to see who could find the smallest and prettiest projectiles. "We didn't take the big ones," he remembers. "We threw them back." Fortunately, he developed a yen for the two to five inch variety as he grew older. When he came across a long, peculiarly grooved specimen, he pocketed it. According to the experts, who visit Alan Smith often these days, that Indian artifact, called a folsom point, is approximately ten thousand years old and very rare to the eastern United States. More commonly found in the high plains area of the Midwest, a folsom point was used to kill wooly mammoths and sabertooth tigers.

Even older are the fossils which oystermen pull up in their patent tongs. Sharks' teeth five inches long and petrified bones come to light after millions of years in the murky depths of the Calvert Sea—now the Chesapeake Bay. Alice Middleton, a former teacher on the island, put together thirty feet of vertebrae from one creature. A waterman's son kept bringing the pieces to science class; the pupils kept putting the pieces together. The children eventually packed their prize in two orange crates and carried it to the Smithsonian Institution in Washington, D.C. Scientists informed the wide-eyed little group that their "dinosaur" was part of a twelve million year old whale.

For the women of Smith Island, fall is a time of harvest. Though gardens were larger at the turn of the century (the island has lost considerable acreage through shore erosion), almost every family carries on the tradition of canning and preserving. In a part of Ewell where the soil is exceptionally fertile, one family's eighth of an acre plot annually yields over forty varieties of fruits and vegetables. Chickens are penned beneath fruit trees, and cucumbers grow up and over the wire cages to save space. Herbs, protected and nurtured for years, have acquired the woody stems of small shrubs. Even the fig trees and pomegranate bushes which grow wild on the island are encouraged to extraordinary yields. A good reason for the luxuriance is the gardener's habit of recycling, in chicken coop and compost heap, all kitchen scraps, weeds, and vegetable refuse.

By late fall, the fruits have been wrapped and placed in attic storage. Potatoes, turnips, onions, and parsnips go in the root cellar covered with sea grass. Relishes, pickles, and preserves are on the pantry shelf. With the advent of the gunning season, a Canada goose or a plump, grain-fed black duck may be hanging from the porch rafters. Thanksgiving is just around the corner.

Once upon a time, the scent of smokehouse hickory wafted through the villages as families stoked fires to cure their butchered hogs. Goats and sheep were rounded up "over to sheep pen gut" for winter use. Now, fresh meats and convenience foods arrive daily. Mrs. Kitching remembers when one cow supplied her neighborhood with milk to drink. Canned milk, brought on the ferryboat, was used for cooking. Today, the cow is long gone. Only the canned milk is still around, an integral part of Smith Island recipes.

Thanksgiving is not quite the same on Smith Island as it was in times gone by. The preparations are less arduous, and there is more food for the effort. People are different, too. Before 1975, the watermen would leave their families in the fall to dredge for oysters in other parts of the Bay. With the resurgence of the oyster in the lower Bay, the men leave their home ports every morning and return every night. Thanksgiving and Christmas are no longer the only meals that families share through the long fall and winter months.

Times have changed, but Smith Island folks are simply more grateful for their comforts. Perhaps the one aspect about Thanksgiving which has endured beyond all others is the blessing of the table. Each family has its own prayer, but the message is the same:

> God, thank you from the bottom of our hearts for bringing us safe home and for taking care of our family. We know you are a living God who protects your children. May we ever be thankful and serve you. In your name we praise you forever. Amen

Rockfish Stuffed with Crabmeat

1	2 1/2 pound rockfish
3/4	pound crabmeat, special
4	strips bacon

Scale and gut fish. Remove head and tail. Wash fish in cold water. Where entrails were, cut straight into fish and down toward tail. Stop one inch short of tail. Fill this pocket with crabmeat which has been picked for extraneous shell. Wrap slices of bacon, bandage fashion, across pocket to secure stuffing. Bake at 350 degrees for one hour.

Baked Stuffed Pork Chops

4	pork chops, 3/4 inch to 1 inch thick, with pocket for stuffing
8	slices bread
1	egg, beaten
1	large onion, diced
1/4	pound butter
2	tablespoons poultry seasoning
	water, enough to moisten bread

Sauté onion in butter. Cube bread and moisten with water. Add egg and poultry seasoning. Mix until well blended then spoon stuffing into each pocket of pork chops. Stand stuffed pork chops up in baking pan (stuffing side up). Cover with aluminum foil. Bake at 350 degrees for 30 minutes. Remove foil and bake at 350 degrees for 30 minutes more.

Corn Fritters

2/3	cup unsifted flour
1	tablespoon baking powder
1/2	teaspoon salt
2	teaspoons sugar
2	eggs, well beaten
1/4	cup butter, melted
1/2	cup evaporated milk
1	teaspoon grated onion
1	16-ounce can whole kernel corn
	vegetable oil, enough to fill frying pan 1/4 inch deep

Sift together dry ingredients, including sugar. Combine eggs, butter, and milk, and blend until uniform. Add onion, corn, and sifted ingredients. Mix well. Heat oil in frying pan. When oil is hot, drop by generous tablespoons into frying pan. Fry each fritter on both sides until golden.

Sauerkraut Salad

1	16-ounce can sauerkraut
1/2	cup diced green and red peppers
1/2	cup grated carrot
1	medium onion, diced
1/2	cup vinegar
1/2	cup oil
1/2	cup sugar

Put sauerkraut in colander and rinse in cold water. Drain well. Combine sauerkraut, peppers, carrot, and onion in bowl. In saucepan, combine vinegar, oil, and sugar, and heat until blended. Pour over vegetables. Refrigerate and serve cold.

Cranberry Nut Mush

4	cups whole fresh cranberries
2	cups sugar
2	cups seedless grapes
1	cup walnut pieces
1	cup chunk pineapple, drained
1/2	pint heavy cream, whipped

Grind cranberries to a mushy consistency. Add sugar and let drain for several hours or overnight in refrigerator. Mix in remaining ingredients. Chill and serve.

White Squash Pudding

3	pounds white, scalloped-edged squash
1/2	cup water
2	tablespoons butter
3	eggs
1 1/2	cups milk
3	tablespoons sugar
3/4	teaspoon salt
3	drops Tabasco Sauce
1	cup bread crumbs
1/2	cup sharp or Parmesan cheese

Slice squash and cook in water and butter until tender (not mushy). Mix together eggs, milk, sugar, salt, and Tabasco Sauce. Pour over squash and add everything to casserole dish. Top with bread crumbs and cheese. Bake at 350 degrees for one-and-one-half hours until firm and brown.

Green Bean Casserole

2	16-ounce cans french cut string beans
3/4	cup milk
1	can cream of mushroom soup
2	slices bacon, diced
1/2	teaspoon salt
	dash pepper

Mix together all ingredients and pour into casserole dish. Bake at 350 degrees for 35 minutes.

Fried Apples

6-8	apples, peeled, sliced, and cored
2	tablespoons butter
1	tablespoon cinnamon
3/4	cup sugar

Melt butter in frying pan. Add apple slices. Sprinkle cinnamon and sugar over apples. Cover and cook over medium heat. Stir occasionally to prevent from sticking. When apples are soft, remove from pan and serve.

Banana Split Cake

2	cups graham cracker crumbs
1/2	cup butter
2	cups powdered sugar
2	eggs
1	teaspoon vanilla
1	20-ounce can crushed pineapple
1	14-ounce package frozen strawberries
4	bananas
	whipped cream (enough for topping)

Mix graham cracker crumbs and butter to pastry consistency and pack on bottom of an 11 × 13 inch baking dish. Beat eggs and slowly add sugar, then vanilla. Spread over crust. Drain pineapple and strawberries. Add pineapple in layer to pie. Add strawberries in layer to pie. Slice bananas lengthwise and layer on top of strawberries. Top generously with whipped cream. Freeze.

Sweet Potato Pie

1	unbaked 9-inch pie crust
3	medium sized sweet potatoes
3/4	cup sugar
1/4	cup butter
	pinch salt
3	eggs, separated
1	tablespoon cornstarch
1	cup evaporated milk
1	teaspoon vanilla
1/2	cup whole milk

Boil sweet potatoes in skins until cooked to seal in sweetness. Remove skins and mash to eliminate lumps. Cream together butter and sugar. Add sweet potatoes, salt, egg yolks, and cornstarch. Slowly add evaporated milk and vanilla. In separate bowl, beat egg whites until stiff and fold into sweet potato mixture. Stir in whole milk. Pour into pie crust. Bake at 400 degrees for 15 minutes, then reduce heat to 350 degrees and bake for 25 minutes. Note: For a variation Mrs. Kitching calls Meringue Sweet Potato Pie, fold 1/2 cup shredded coconut into sweet potato mixture instead of egg whites. Use egg whites as a meringue topping. To make meringue topping, beat egg whites until stiff, slowly add 6 teaspoons of sugar while beating. Spread meringue over already baked pie (follow baking instructions for sweet potato pie), and bake at 350 degrees until meringue is golden.

Have you ever heard tell of pompano in the Chesapeake Bay, or
shrimp the size and succulence of the Outer Banks' finest, or three
hundred pound sturgeon that grow nine feet long? Did you ever see
a ship's hold full of fish called "swellin' toads" that inflate like
balloons and taste like chicken; or come upon a fishing net that
corralled a record-sized bull shark?

> That was a brand new net we had up to Sagey Point. I
> don't think she'd been out a week 'n we landed there to
> her one mornin' 'n there weren't nuthin' in her but this
> great ole big bull shark. He'd gone roight through the
> front of the pound 'n took net 'n all roight with him.
> Even with that big hole there where he went through,
> he wouldn't even offer to go out 'o that. He'd just stay
> there 'n circle around. He was in there by hisself—if
> there was anything else in there, he'd just eat it up. Yup,
> there weren't nuthin' but him; that's all there was."

The shrimp Smith Islanders catch, entirely by accident in crab
scraping nets, are packed away in the deep freeze until an accumu-
lation makes a meal. Not so the Brobdingnagian harvests from
their fishing nets. Remarkable catches usually land in the fish
markets of Baltimore and New York.

> That sturgeon took me 'n Ernest both to get him on the
> stern. When we did pull him up on there, he weighed
> three hundred pounds. We got him to Crisfield 'n a feller
> that bought fish looked him over 'n he said he'd give us
> fifty dollars for him. We talked it over. "Yeah, well, we'll
> letcha have him," we said. We let him have him for fifty
> 'n he carried him there to Baltimore 'n that's exactly
> what he got for him.

The Maryland Department of Natural Resources has no record of
pompano in the Chesapeake Bay, but for two weeks during the
summer of 1966, Elmer Evans and Ernest Kitching hauled about
one hundred pounds of pompano out of Tangier Sound.

> "I had no idea they'd be up this far," recounted Elmer
> Evans, "Because they're a tropical fish." The first
> mornin' we had seventeen, and they'd go a pound 'n a
> half each. I guess we caught pretty close to a hundred all
> together. The first time we caught 'em we sold 'em to a
> feller in Crisfield. We told him they were pompano.
> "No," he said, "They're irontails." Irontail looks exactly

like a pompano only he's got these spurs on his tail like a mackerel. Pompano's got a wide, flat tail with no spurs on the edge of it.

"Well," I said, "I'll find out tomorrow [if they're pompano] when I ship any more I catch to New York." So, he give us thirty-five cent a pound for 'em that day. When we got a return from New York, that Crisfield feller wanted to see it. He said, "I guess you never will sell me another one will you?" We got ninety cent a pound in New York for 'em. "Found out they were pompano alroight."

Smith Island fisherman can be blasé about nature's wonders. They see more in a season than most folks discover in a lifetime. One man hardly glanced at the beached husk of a massive drumfish, "Bay grows 'em upward of a hundred pound," was the extent of his enthusiasm. Take him away from his vocation, however, and you will learn his love of it. "Ever made a livin' fishin', it's something you never get out of your blood," said a retired pound netter. "I'd rather do it than eat."

Years ago, Smith Islanders only fished to eat. Lillian Marshall can remember when her father would go fall fishing for sea trout. "He'd come home 'n scale 'em, clean 'em, salt 'em, 'n put 'em in wooden tubs to last through the winter." When refrigeration created a fishing industry on the Bay, the men simply engineered bigger nets to accommodate the demand. Today, they erect huge pound or stake nets along shore to snare schooling fish; they cast floating nets (called drift or gill nets) overboard; and they employ the hand line, a pastime that still puts supper on the table.

A commercial fishing license is good from January 1 until December 31, but Smith Island fishermen concentrate their efforts on the period between early spring and late fall. It is then that anadromous fish migrate to and from their spawning grounds at the head of the Bay. Spring brings greater quantities of fish, but fall allows "a better chance at 'em" as they fatten up in the shallows on their way down the Bay. Spring runs of herring, shad, and alewives glut the market. The bigger, fatter fish of fall fetch better prices.

Rockfish, black bass, mackerel, sea trout, speckled trout, flounder, bluefish, drumfish, white perch, Norfolk spot, hardheads, and butterfish are plentiful around Smith Island right up until the nor'westers of late fall send them streaming for deeper, warmer water. No one knows from year to year how they will run, or if they will run at all. Certain species have all but disappeared from the Bay. Yellow perch are depleted. Swelling toads, also called blowfish or sea squabs, were a promising fishery until 1971 when their prodigious numbers vanished. Smith Islanders mourn their passing. Overheard many times around the island is the query, "Where'd the swellin' toads go at?" The frequent reply, "Only the Lord knows," has lately been superseded by speculation. "They went to Japan," said one old fisherman. "I hear-ed they got hardheads over there, too, and didn't know what they were."

Fish are capricious, but if anyone can read them, Smith Islanders can. Elmer Evans outsmarts rockfish like this: "Go late of an evening off a bank on the first quarter of the flood tide with the wind rollin' 'round to westward." He says to get to know tidal changes in several spots because fish feed easiest in the slack water starting an ebb or a flood tide. Of paramount importance is his warning to watch the weather. "If you see a squall comin' up, run. You never know what's in 'em."

Frances Kitching proffers tips on the preparation of fish. Her cardinal rule: be sure the fish is fresh. To ascertain freshness, lift the gill slit. If the membrane is red, the fish is fresh within three days. If the membrane is pink, the fish is probably a week old. Fish begins to taste "fishy" three days after it has been caught.

Use a long, thin, flexible blade honed to razor sharpness for filleting. You can get closer to the bone with it. Because flounder is so slippery, Elmer Evans suggests driving a nail through its head to facilitate filleting. The method is humane; flounder are slow to die and are usually skinned alive.

If bluefish seems too strong a fish for your taste, try removing the dark dorsal (oil gland) meat when filleting. And, if you catch the fish yourself, be sure to cut the blue's throat to bleed it. The fish will be sweeter.

Smith Islanders have an ingenious method of freezing fish which preserves flavor. First, they prepare the fish by scaling, gutting, and removing the head and tail. The fish may be filleted or left whole. Then, they place the fish inside a plastic freezer container and fill it, covering the fish, with cold water. Most fish will freeze better in this fashion, as will soft shell crabs. Rockfish are one of the few fish which stay juicy through freezing just wrapped in wax paper and sealed in tin foil. Wrap up shad and put it in the freezer without cleaning it.

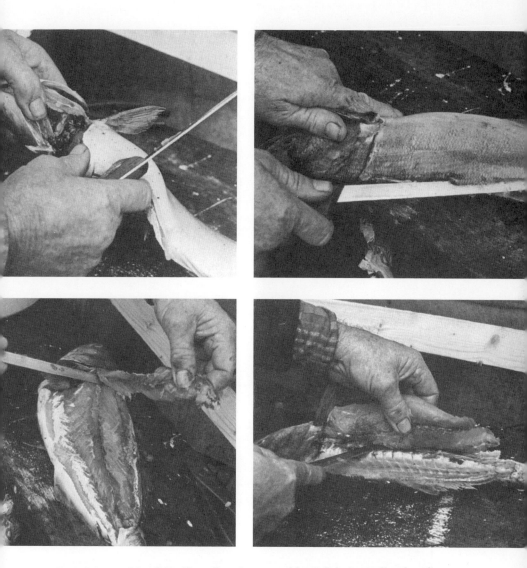

Preparing a bluefish: *Top*. Cut throat to bleed fish immediately after catching it. With sharp fileting knife, make shallow lengthwise cut dorsally, ventrally, and crosswise below fins (which are below gills); then peel off skin. *Bottom*. With skin removed, the oil glands on both sides of fish will appear as dark strips. Cut out oil glands as shown and discard. Filet the fish as close to the backbone as possible.

65

Baked, Stuffed Fish

1	2 1/2 - 3 pound flounder, bluefish, rockfish, or croaker
3/4	pound crabmeat, regular
4	strips bacon

Scale and gut fish. Remove head and tail. Wash fish in cold water. For bluefish, rockfish, and croaker, cut a pocket into fish (for stuffing) via the side previously gutted. Cut straight into fish above backbone and then down toward tail. Stop one inch short of tail. Fill pocket with crabmeat which has been picked for extraneous shell. For flounder, before making pocket, cut away bony ridge which runs along both sides of fish. To make pocket in flounder, enter where head was. Stop one inch short of tail. Fill with well-picked crabmeat. Wrap slices of bacon, bandage fashion, across pocket to secure stuffing. Bake at 350 degrees one hour.

Baked Rockfish with Potatoes

1	2-3 pound rockfish, scaled, with head, tail, and innards removed
1	large onion
5	medium sized potatoes
	salt and pepper to taste
4	thin slices salt pork or 3 tablespoons bacon grease
2	tablespoons flour
1 1/2	cups water

Peel the potatoes and cut into rounds. Dice the onion. Put the potatoes and onion into a baking dish with the fish. Salt and pepper to taste. Add the salt pork or bacon grease, arranging around the fish. Mix 2 tablespoons of flour in 1 1/2 cups water and pour over the fish, onion, potatoes, and salt pork. Cover the baking dish, and bake at 350 degrees until the rockfish is brown. Baking time is about one hour.

Baked Sea Trout

1	2-3 pound sea trout, filleted
	salt and pepper to taste
1	large onion
1/2	stick butter

Place fish, open face, in baking dish. Salt and pepper liberally. Cut up onion into rounds and lay over fish. Pour melted butter over top. Bake at 350 degrees for 45 minutes.

Broiled Bluefish

1	bluefish (any size) filleted
	butter (1 tablespoon per pound of fish)
	Worcestershire Sauce (1/2 teaspoon per pound of fish)
	lemon juice to taste

Melt butter in saucepan. Add Worcestershire Sauce and lemon juice. Broil fish, 10 minutes to the pound, at 325 degrees and baste with butter sauce every 10 minutes.

Broiled Fish in Mayonnaise Sauce

3 1/2	pound Flounder or sea trout, filleted
	salt and pepper to taste
1/2	cup mayonnaise
1	tablespoon Worcestershire Sauce
2	teaspoons lemon juice
1	tablespoon Old Bay Seasoning

Wash fillets in cold water. Salt and pepper to taste. Place scale side down in broiler. Combine mayonnaise, Worcestershire Sauce, and lemon juice. Spread over fish fillets. Sprinkle Old Bay Seasoning over top. Broil, two rack settings below broiler, for 20 minutes.

Broiled Flounder

1	flounder (any size)
	butter (1 tablespoon per pound of fish)
	salt and pepper to taste

Broil fish, scales side down, on the lowest rack setting. Baste with butter, and season with salt and pepper. After 15 minutes, turn fish over. Baste with butter and season with salt and pepper. Broil for 15 more minutes, then serve.

Herring or Shad Roe

1	pint roe
1	cup self-rising flour
	salt and pepper to taste
1/2	cup vegetable oil

Wash roe in cold water. Drain. Combine salt, pepper, and flour. Dredge roe in seasoned flour. Heat oil in skillet. When hot, add roe. Fry on both sides until golden. Serves four.

Stewed Rockfish or Croaker

1	3 pound rockfish or croaker, scaled, with head, tail and innards removed
4	thin slices salt pork, 2 inches long
1	tablespoon flour
	salt and pepper to taste
2	cups water
1	medium onion, sliced
4	potatoes, sliced

Cut fish in small 2 to 3 inch pieces, steak fashion, perpendicular to backbone. Fry salt pork and remove rind. Brown flour in remaining grease. Slowly add water to make a paste and add fish, onion, and potatoes. Salt and pepper to taste. Cover and cook over medium heat for 45 minutes. Always remember that fish falls apart, when baked or stewed, after the first 20 minutes. Let the fish cook for 25 more minutes and it will become firm.

Fried Fish

1   2-2 1/2 pound fish, filleted
1   cup flour
      salt and pepper to taste
      vegetable oil, enough to fill frying pan to depth of
        1/2-inch

Any of the following fish are excellent fried: mackerel; drumfish; perch; butterfish; flounder; Norfolk spot; sea trout; rockfish; black bass; sea squab. Wash fish fillets in cold water. Dredge in flour seasoned with salt and pepper. Fry in hot oil on both sides, at medium heat, until golden.

Boiled Codfish

2   pound dried codfish
6   medium potatoes
2   medium onions
1/4   pound salt pork, sliced

Soak codfish overnight in cold water. Drain in the morning. Add fresh water to cover. Scrub potatoes, and add to water. Bring water to boil, and cook with a cover on the pot until potatoes are tender. Put fish on a platter and garnish with sliced onion rounds. Fry up salt pork and pour grease over fish and onions. Note: To make codfish cakes, mash leftover fish and potatoes. Add 3 tablespoons of flour to each pound of fish and potatoes. Form cakes and fry in a skillet in a little vegetable oil.

Boiled Black Bass, Norfolk Spot or Sea Trout

1   1 1/2 pound fish, filleted
      salt and pepper to taste
2   tablespoons bacon grease

Wash fish fillets in cold water. Place in pan and cover with cold water. Bring to a boil. Boil for five minutes. Remove fish and season with salt and pepper. Spoon hot bacon grease over fish and serve.

Smith Islanders "go gunnin'" for ducks and geese. They trap otter, mink, muskrat, and fox. Occasionally, they land a deer swimming across the Bay. Alan Smith's daddy hauled a young white tailed buck into his skiff three miles out in the Bay, then brought him home and lodged him in the backyard for the rest of his natural life. A lone beaver paddling up a local swash during the spring of 1980 encountered a less enthusiastic reception. The Maryland State Department of Natural Resources sent him packing back to the mainland. Explained Michael Harrison, "There ain't enough trees here to share with a beaver."

Before the first Evanses, Tylers, Marshalls, and Bradshaws learned to eat crabs and rake oysters from the Chesapeake, they were subsisting on fish and game. The subsistence level was hardly meager. Captain John Smith, sailing through the region in 1608, purportedly dipped a ship's skillet overboard and came up with fish for supper. Fish and fowl, he concluded in the ship's log, are abundant in the isles of the Chesapeake in any season. The myriad Indian arrowheads washing up on the island's shores substantiate Smith's boasts of a "fruitful and delightsome land." Extensive hunting grounds, today mostly inundated by the Bay, antedated John Smith by thousands of years. The big game, says one islander, only disappeared in the early twentieth century. He has a piece of caribou antler to prove it.

Old timer Paul Marshall is an authority on the island's wildlife. He has hunted, killed, eaten, stuffed, carved, and painted it. Although ducks and geese are his forte, he will proffer information on any and all species that inhabit the marshes. To hear him tell about the red fox, you would never guess some of the best furs in the state originate there. "Now who in the devil wants fox in a huntin' area? They eat up any dern thing they come across." On mink: "It'd be hard to say how many there are. They're harder to catch than muskrat, and they are a nuisance because they kill muskrat." The islanders are partial to muskrat. From early winter to late spring dozens of stretched pelts hang on clotheslines and dry in backyard outhouses all over the island. The furs have traditionally been a source of extra income and the meat, stewed or fried, is a well known Eastern shore delicacy.

Otters have made a come back in the past ten years. They fascinate local hunters. Paul Marshall recounts one of his only experiences with them. "Last summer, I ran up the shore here, an' I saw this thing ahead of me on the water. I thought it was a great big fish but it wasn't. It was an otter. I watched it for ten minutes. It wouldn't leave. It'd just come up, playin', to fifteen feet of me. Oh—I could've killed it twenty times, but I wouldn'a done it. But I counted!"

According to Paul Marshall, there are not enough people on Smith Island to disturb the environment. "People here are more in danger of gettin' extinct than the animals," he asserts. "Not more 'n ten people go gunnin'. Game wardens think everyone does." What the game wardens watch, to the everlasting irritation of every man, woman, and child on the island, is the duck hunting.

Duck hunting is a subject best not broached without considerable forethought. At worst, folks might think that you are a game warden. At best, they will resent your stirring up memories of a once cherished pastime. For generations, watermen helped themselves to the winged bounty in their front yards. Then the government appropriated a large portion of the island's northern marshland for a wildlife refuge. "Now," says a man who put away his gun four years ago, "There's nuthin' to talk about. Government came in 'n gobbled up the land. Once you'd be guaranteed a kill. Now, they've bottled us all up . . . "

There are fines for killing out of season; for killing too many; and for killing protected species. A canvasback will cost five hundred dollars. A swan goes for a thousand. Once, men sold their kill to restaurants. Nine foot long punt guns could bring down a boatload at one firing. "You gotta shoot one o' them just exactly," says Paul Marshall, the last man on the island to use one.

> "There were loifetime occasions when you could bring down (a boatload) . . . now, my grandfather done it all his loife an' he said twelve geese were as many as he killed at one time. I remember three guns together once killed one hundred and eight ducks."

The days of the punt gun are forty years gone, but the wardens drop in frequently to make sure they do not return.

Just like the mainland police whose stealthy arrival is disclosed by the first ticket they issue, game wardens sneak up on the islanders. One undercover official made friends with a Rhodes Point man. He came out to the island, ate dinner, and stayed overnight with the family. He also purchased some ducks from the man. Shortly thereafter, the Smith Islander was arrested, sent to court, and heavily fined for the illegal possession of ducks.

To add to the unanimous anger and frustration folks feel about gunning, the bottom grass on which the ducks feed has mysteriously died back in recent years, thus discouraging all but diving

72

ducks from the area, and many of these are protected. Since the islanders are not allowed to entice wildfowl with corn, many have given up and shelved their guns. Lamented a former hunter, "'Used to be a family could have a nice Thanksgiving, but now you cain't even have that."

It is small wonder, then, that Mrs. Kitching's repertory of wildfowl recipes is so scant. You might say it has atrophied from disuse. Furthermore, she does not serve wildfowl to her guests for that, too, is against the law.

GAME RECIPES

Pan Browned Wild Duck

1	2- 3 1/2 pound wild duck (pin-tailed or black duck)
1	cup water
1	teaspoon vinegar
1	medium onion, optional
1	large turnip
5	medium potaotes
	salt and pepper to taste

Soak the duck overnight in salt water. The duck should be roughly 70 degrees or room temperature when you start to cook with it. Place the whole duck, breast down, in a large roasting pan. (The size of the roasting pan can vary with the size of the duck.) Add the one cup of water, cover and bring to a full boil. To counteract too gamey a flavor, add the 1 teaspoon of vinegar and 1 medium onion to the one cup of water when browning the bird. Wait 10 minutes for the water to boil off, then brown the bird on all sides in the remaining grease. When the duck is as brown as you like it, cover it completely with water. Add salt and pepper to taste and cover. Cook until tender. Midway through the cooking, add the sliced pieces of turnip and the peeled potatoes. Cooking time will vary with the size of the bird. When the bird is done, a fork should be able to penetrate to the breastbone.

Stewed Goose

1   goose, any size
2   cups water, plus additional water to cover
3   medium turnips, sliced
4   medium potatoes, peeled and sliced
       dumplings (recipe to follow)
       salt and pepper to taste

Pick goose and remove the innards. Cut up the goose, but leave the breast whole. Place the pieces in a roasting pan, add two cups of water, cover, and cook over medium heat until the water evaporates. A rich goose fat will replace the water in the bottom of the roasting pan. Brown the pieces on all sides in the fat. When sufficiently browned, cover the fowl with water. Salt and pepper to taste. Cook covered until tender. Add sliced turnips and potatoes and cook covered for ten minutes or until the vegetables are tender. Water may be replenished as needed. Remove the fowl and the vegetables, and keep warm. Drop dumplings into the juices. Cover the roasting pan, and cook for seven minutes. Remove the dumplings, and keep warm. To make gravy, dissolve two tablespoons of cornstarch in 1/2 cup cold water. Add it to approximately four cups of pan drippings in the roasting pan. Stir and cook over medium heat until thickened.

Dumplings

1   cup flour
3/4   teaspoon salt
1   teaspoon baking powder
1/4-1/3   cup water

Sift flour, salt and baking powder. Add water slowly and knead to form a dough. Sprinkle flour on waxed paper, and roll out dough to 1/4 inch thickness. Cut out dumplings with a knife or cookie cutter in the shape and size desired and cook as directed.

Fried Wild Duck

1	2-3 pound wild duck
1/2	cup flour
1/4	cup white cornmeal
1/2	cup vegetable oil
	salt and pepper to taste

Pick the duck and remove the innards. Cut up in pieces as you would a frying chicken. Soak the pieces in salt water overnight in the refrigerator. Drain, when ready to use, and pat dry. Combine flour, cornmeal, salt, and pepper in a bowl. Heat the vegetable oil in a frying pan. When the oil is hot, dip the duck pieces quickly into the oil, just enough to coat the surface. Dredge each oil-coated piece in the seasoned flour-cornmeal mixture. Return the pieces to the hot oil and fry on all sides until golden. Lower the temperature and simmer for one half hour or until duck pieces are tender.

CHAPTER THREE

Winter

All the credit cards in Christendom will not buy merchandise in Smith Island's general stores. The storekeepers in those vintage emporia honor a more exclusive form of credit—they have to know you. As for bill collection, it is not uncommon to see a sign posted in the front window reading, "Those who haven't paid bills in three months, please pay up."

As the only men on the island who do not follow the water (besides the preacher and postmaster), the four storekeepers spend a lot of time with their customers. Their six day-a-week business of importing mainland supplies twice daily, via ferryboat, may curtail their own jawing, but they take great pains to insure that everyone else entering the premises loses hours to the pleasant art of conversation.

During the winter, a well stoked potbellied stove commands front stage center in Tylerton's expansive one room general store. The woodbox is full. Benches, stools, and chairs at ringside are usually full too. At the few tables, contests of pitch, pinochle, and dominoes are in progress; and, in the wings, a small army of feminine help takes orders for breakfast, lunch, dinner, and snacks. Depending upon weather conditions, the watermen are in for an hour, a day, or an evening of yarn telling.

Talk is cursory at first, about the weather, how the oystering is going, whose mast snapped in yesterday's squall. Yarn telling will not begin until a practiced raconteur whets everyone's appetite. Before the advent of television, everyone in the circle was an accomplished storyteller. Nine swivel chairs in one general store were reserved each night by the "old heads." Cheeseboxes full of sand served as cuspidors to accommodate overworked jaws. The younger crowd sat on benches and listened, or they sat on benches in the store down the road to create their own yarns. Seventy-one year old Alex Kellam learned the yarns of his elders from a place on the bench. Today, he commands a chair and an audience when he visits any general store on the island. Alex tells his stories with all the flair and authenticity of the old days. He is one of the last to remember when there was hardly any transportation to the island. His accent preserves what has been described as Smith Island's vestigial Elizabethan speech. Here is a story about a captain with an inexperienced mate:

> This captain was going up the Bay and his mate wasn't too experienced a boatman. They had sailed all day and it was well into the night. 'Bout two o'clock in the morning, the captain got sleepy. He said to his mate, "You're gonna have to steer this boat so I can go down and get a couple of hours sleep." When the mate took her, the captain said, "See that star up ahead? You hold her for that star." With that, the captain went down and went to sleep. He slept longer than he expected. He woke with a start, jumped out on deck, and said to his mate, "Are you still holdin' for that star?!" Said the mate, "Hell no, cap'n. I passed that one hours ago."

Recalcitrant crew members were dear to every waterman's heart unless, of course, he happened to be saddled with one. Alex tells a yarn about a stubborn Irishman.

> This schooner was running down the Bay with a deck-load of lumber. She had an Irishman up forward as a lookoutsman. Along about two o'clock in the morning, the Irishman come aft and said to the captain, "Cap'n, I'm tired. Let's go to bed." Captain said, "You go forward, Pat. Take care of your end—I'll take care of mine back here." With that, Pat went forward, grumbling to himself. In two hours, he was back with the same story. And, of course, this time the captain was really mad. He told him, in no uncertain terms, "Pat, you get the hell up forward and take care of your end. I'll take care of mine back here." So, Pat went forward and let the anchor go. The anchor come tight. Half the boatload of lumber went overboard, and the schooner almost capsized.
>
> "Pat, what the hell have you done!?" yelled the captain. "I've anchored my end," Pat yelled back. "You can do what you damn well please with yours!"

Some say you will hear the best yarn telling during the winter on Smith Island. "Any other time, they'll just be tellin' lies," chuckles

78

Morris Goodwin Marsh. The men tell their best stories when treacherous weather brings everyone closer. Winter is the most dangerous time of year. Oyster tonging is no harder than crabbing, but weather conditions on the Chesapeake Bay are more risky in winter. Days, sometimes weeks, will pass before captains can venture from the lee of village harbors. Ask any one of these stalwart men what they fear about being on the water in the middle of winter and you will be surprised at the answer. No one indulges in specific fears like drowning, being lost on the Bay, or having the family patent tonging/crab-potting workboat sink at mooring. A dozen such fears are omnipresent in the mind of a proficient waterman. "Fear? This is what you fear," says Morris Goodwin Marsh, "when you ain't got the drive to go (out there) and you gotta go for to make anything." Elmer Evans put it more succinctly. He called it "losing your nerve."

Yarns are an outlet for these men, and sometimes, a source of instruction. Former Tangier Sound Watermen's Association President, Jennings Evans, explains, "Any crisis that comes up has been dealt with years back, and that's how these stories came into being. Some of them are true. The majority got a little truth to 'em. Some have been polished up to make the laugh even better." During the winter of 1977, one old yarn got resurrected and retold weekly in the general stores. It helped the islanders through a similar crisis. When anyone started taking his situation seriously, he had only to listen to the story of the freeze of 1918 to laugh away his troubles.

> They were froze up to Holland's Island one time, and they were getting low on food. There was one piece of meat left on the whole island. The man who owned it tied a string to it and passed it from family to family so everyone could cook their beans with it. The meat came to the last man on the island before it was to go back up the way and start at the beginning again. Well, darned if that man didn't cook the meat with black-eyed peas. He ruined it! When the rest of the island folks found out what he had done, they started building a gallows to hang him!

> Well, they got that gallows built, and just as they were ready to hang him . . . the freeze broke.

For seven weeks during the winter of 1977, Smith Islanders were locked in the clutches of a freeze that sank boats, burst pipes, and cut off all regular traffic to the mainland. No one walked to Cris-

81

field like they did in 1936. A ferocious stretch of open water called the "Puppy Hole" cut one hundred feet deep through the middle of Tangier Sound—the prospects of dragging a skiff there to ford it were not inviting.

Most folks stayed put and made light of their plight. Kids skated and went sliding down forty-foot "icebergs" heaved up on the Bayside beach. Tylerton residents fed corn to fifteen thousand starving ducks and geese. The resident preacher maintained his Sunday circuit of the three island churches, in spite of the ice surrounding Tylerton. Not liking his trek, but game, he announced that "walking on the water" would figure well in a future sermon.

No one worked, and no one earned money. But, by all accounts, they spent the nicest time in the world visiting each other, having parties, and hanging around in the general stores. How did they live? "Helicopters!" declared one boy. Helicopters imported groceries, fuel oil, and repairmen, and exported the ailing. No one went hungry or lived on beans.

Among the television and newspaper reporters covering the situation was a man who stayed a month at Kitching's Inn. His description of the meals available during that period rivals any yarn the old heads will tell about the freeze of '77. Who would believe a person could enjoy some of the most delicious cooking on the Chesapeake Bay during one of the worst freezes in history?

WINTER MENU

Oyster Stew

1	pint standard oysters with liquor
	dumplings (recipe to follow)
1 1/2	cups water (including oyster liquor)
	salt and pepper to taste
1	small onion, diced finely
1	cup evaporated milk
3	tablespoons butter

Cook oysters in 1 1/2 cups liquor-water until edges of oysters curl. Pinch tiny dumplings from dough and drop into cooking oysters. Add diced onions and cook over medium heat for about 15 minutes or until dumplings are no longer doughy. Heat milk, water, and butter. When hot, pour into oyster stew.

Serve at once.

Dumplings

1/2 cup flour
1/2 teaspoon salt
1/2 teaspoon baking powder
1/8 cup water

Sift flour, salt, and baking powder. Add water, a little at a time, and knead to form dough. Pinch off tiny dumpling balls 1/4 inch round for oyster stew.

Oyster Supreme

1 pint standard oysters with liquor
1 package (or 40) soda crackers
3 tablespoons butter
1 small onion, grated
1 cup grated mozzarella cheese
salt and pepper to taste
1/2-1 cup evaporated milk or heavy cream

Grease a 1 1/2 quart casserole with one tablespoon butter. Crumble 3/4 of package (or 30) crackers and spread evenly on bottom of casserole dish. Place oysters in a layer atop crackers. Salt and pepper to taste. Grate onion over oysters. Crumble remaining crackers over oysters. Dab with remaining butter. Pour oyster liquor into a one-cup measure and add evaporated milk or cream to fill. Pour the liquid uniformly over top. Spread grated mozzarella cheese evenly over top. Bake at 350 degrees for 35 to 40 minutes.

Chicken Divan

1 pound chicken breasts, cooked and diced
2 10-ounce boxes frozen broccoli, cooked and drained
1 cup mayonnaise
1 teaspoon lemon juice
1 10 1/2-ounce can cream of chicken soup
1 10 1/2-ounce can cream of celery soup
croutons, at least 1 cup

Mix mayonnaise, lemon juice, soups, and diced chicken in a bowl. Pour over broccoli in a 1 1/2-quart casserole. Top with croutons and bake at 325 degrees for 45 minutes.

Pineapple Sauce Casserole

4	apples, cored, skinned and diced
1	20-ounce can crushed pineapple
2	eggs, slightly beaten
1/2	cup sugar
6	slices bread, crusts removed, diced
1/4	cup butter, melted

Combine apples and pineapple. Stir in beaten eggs, sugar, and 2/3 of the diced bread. Pour mixture into a shallow baking dish. Dot with remaining pieces of bread and pour melted butter uniformly over all. Bake at 350 degrees for 30 to 40 minutes.

Vegetable Jello Salad

1	package lime jello
1	cup hot water
2	cups shredded cabbage
1	cup shredded carrots
1	small onion, diced
1	medium sized cucumber, diced
3	tablespoons vinegar
1/2	teaspoon salt

Dissolve jello in water. Add vinegar and salt. Cool slightly. Add the vegetables and place in refrigerator for one hour to gel.

Sweet Potato Soufflé

3	medium sweet potatoes
3	tablespoons brown sugar
1/3	cup butter
2	eggs, separated
3/4	cup milk, heated
1/2	teaspoon salt
1 1/2	teaspoons grated lemon rind
3/4	cup shredded coconut

Boil sweet potatoes with skins on until cooked. Remove skins and mash to eliminate lumps. Cream together sugar, butter, and sweet potatoes. Add egg yolks and blend. Add heated milk and salt. Beat until light. Stir in coconut and lemon rind. In a separate bowl, beat egg whites until stiff peaks form, then fold into potato mixture. Pour into ungreased baking dish and bake at 375 degrees for one hour or until top is slightly browned.

Corn Spoon Bread

1	15 1/2-ounce can cream style corn
1	cup self-rising cornmeal
1	teaspoon baking powder
1	cup sour cream
2	eggs, well beaten
1/2	cup vegetable oil

Mix together corn, cornmeal, baking powder, sour cream, and eggs. Heat oil until hot and pour slowly into corn bread batter. Pour mixture into 1 1/2-quart baking dish. Bake at 375 degrees for 35 to 40 minutes.

Collard Greens for Six

1/2	pound salt pork
2 1/2	pound collard greens
1 1/2	quarts water
	salt to taste

Hopefully, you have planted collard greens at the end of August so you are ready to harvest them in the middle of winter. The more frosts the greens are subjected to, the sweeter they taste.

Bring 1 1/2 quarts of water to a boil. Cut salt pork in slices semi-attached to the rind and drop into boiling water. Add salt and collard greens to water. Cook until wilted and tender, about 15 minutes.

French Apple Pie

1	9-inch unbaked pie shell
2	cups peeled, sliced apples
2	tablespoons flour
1/8	teaspoon salt
1	teaspoon cinnamon
1/4	teaspoon nutmeg
3/4	cup sugar
1	cup sour cream
1	egg, slightly beaten
1	teaspoon vanilla

Sift together dry ingredients (including sugar). Blend sour cream, egg, and vanilla and add to dry ingredients. Mix well and pour over sliced apples. Stir the apples in mixture and coat well. Turn apples into pie shell. Bake at 350 degrees for 15 minutes. Then remove from oven and top with the following ingredients combined to make a crumb mixture:

1/3	cup sugar
1/3	cup flour
1	teaspoon cinnamon
1/4	cup butter, at room temperature

Bake at 350 degrees for one hour.

Cracker Pudding, A Skipjack Recipe

30	unsalted soda crackers
1	cup water
2	eggs, beaten
	pinch salt
2	cups sugar
1	teaspoon vanilla
1	13-ounce can evaporated milk
1	cup whole milk
1/4	cup butter, melted

Put crackers in a bowl and soak in one cup water until soft. Add eggs, salt, sugar, and vanilla. Stir to make uniform mixture. Add evaporated milk and whole milk. The pudding is very thin, as it is supposed to be. Pour butter into a 9 x 13-inch baking dish, and pour pudding over it. Bake at 350 degrees for 45 minutes to one hour.

If you want to make a waterman laugh in the middle of a cold, hard winter of oystering, ask him about the sex life of an oyster. "Oh my land," says Captain Ernest Kitching. "Now, there's a story. But you ain't gonna get it from me."

You ain't gonna get it from marine biologists, either, because *Crassostrea virginica* has everyone guessing. During its natural fifteen to twenty year life span, America's East Coast species of oyster enjoys a change of sex, at least once. The tendency is to be male while young and female for the balance. Exactly when the metamorphosis occurs depends upon the individual, but three to four years is a given average. By then, most *Crassostrea* youngsters are three inches long and fair game for man's dinner table. In the Chesapeake Bay, the greatest natural oyster producing area in the world, an oyster does not stay female for long. She gets eaten.

European oysters compound the guesswork. Not only do they change sex, they change sex with a frequency that can only connote enjoyment. Gleeful, too, is their habit of sheltering offspring in the shell for a time after giving birth. Anyone trespassing on the molluscan domicile between the months of May and August gets a mouthful of grit for his troubles. In Europe, you do not want to eat oysters in the summertime; hence, the origin of the ancient maxim: "It is unseasonable and unwholesome in all months that do not have an R in their name to eat an oyster."

In America, the R month maxim does not apply since American oysters expel their eggs from the shell. Why, then, do we perpetuate the myth? "It's the people," Smith Islanders assert. "They think you can't eat 'em then. But oysters are good anytime of the year. Onliest time we don't eat 'em is when they're spawning; when it's real hot. They taste the same, just not so plump."

The R month myth is not entirely responsible for squelching the national oyster appetite. State fisheries laws nip the market in its perennial bud. Maryland law limits oyster harvesting in public beds from September 15 through March 31 each year. So, unless your oysters come from state leased private beds, chances are you will never taste a summer oyster.

"There's sense to it," Captain Edward Harrison avers. "Oysters stay in one place all their lives. If you don't protect 'em, they could be cleaned out." A veteran waterman of forty years, Harrison started culling oysters right out of the fourth grade. By fourteen, he was a deckhand aboard an oyster dredging skipjack for the winter season. During the Depression, he and his brother bought their own skipjack and between seasons educated the likes of

Walter Cronkite and *National Geographic* magazine to the ways of the water.

"There's a lot of worry to oystering," Captain Edward explains.

> Many a night I lay under that sail and worried about making enough money for my crew to support their families; about learnin' the crew to cull the oysters. Marine police come alongside, they'll cull every oyster in a bushel basket. More 'n five percent under three inches and you get fined. And you take the weather. Many a cold night I didn't know if I could get the frozen sail down. Come on a blow, she could capsize.

The *Ruby G. Ford* was more than a boat to him, more than a friend. "Being on a boat all your life, that boat becomes a part of you. 'Helps raise your family. For her size, she was about as smart a boat as there was on the Bay." Today, the skipjacks are gone from Smith Island, abandoned or sold to other captains on the Eastern Shore. Motor powered patent tonging boats with their hydraulic machinery and crew of two have replaced the graceful six-man sailboats. The days of dredging for oysters with the winter wind screaming through the foresail and the dredges raking the Bay bottom may be over but the killingly hard work remains the same.

At the crack of dawn, patent tongers lower the gear for the first "lick" of the day. A man knows he is "on oysters" when a chain dragged across the bottom "feels like a briarpatch." The briarpatch is, more often than not, located on any one of a thousand "oyster rocks" in the Bay. Maryland's forty-five hundred licensed oystermen call them rocks but, in reality, they are oyster bars miles long, in places, and centuries thick with growth. Their names—Turtle Egg, Graveyard, Snake Rip, Old Woman, The "Holler"—are old, of mostly untraceable origin, and rife with waterman's whimsy. "Ice cream cones" are the hard-to-find little hills of oysters which draw adventurous loners like Elmer Evans. "At the rocks," he explains, "you're guaranteed five to fifteen bushels a day. Lookin' for hills, you may get forty bushels. You may get two." The limit nowadays is twenty-five bushels per man per day, but even without catching the limit everyday, a Smith Island oysterman could feed sixteen thousand people dinner with the fruits of one season's labor.

By sunset, if high seas have not earlier called a halt to the tonging operation, every boat must sell its catch to the nearest buy boat. One of the small pleasures of the difficult work is sampling the product ice cold off the bottom. There are few Smith Island men

Shucking an oyster: *Top.* Hold against stationary surface with left hand and feel with knife (in right hand) for oyster's soft spot or "mouth." Run shucking knife straight in to the center or heart of oyster to slacken muscles. *Bottom.* Twist knife to pry shells apart and sever muscle attaching top shell. Discard top shell, sever muscle attaching oyster to bottom shell and turn oyster and liquor out into container.

91

who do not enjoy shucking one on the spot and sliding it down *sans* garnishment. The East Coast oyster is, after all, one of nature's nearly complete foods, with less cholesterol than many varieties of fish and all kinds of meat. In fact, The National Heart and Lung Institute, one of the national institutes of health, has added oysters to its low cholesterol diet. The protein content is legendary. Four ounces of oysters, cooked or raw, supplies half of man's daily protein requirement.

Smith Islanders will be the first to tell you how much better Chincoteague oysters taste than Chesapeake Bay oysters. "Just as salt as pickle and much better raw. Save the Bay oysters for cooking." That is generous advice from men who get a good deal less money for their product than oystermen of Chincoteague Bay. What most people do not realize, however, is that the oysters caught today in the Chesapeake Bay may be Chincoteague Bay's finest two months hence. Indigenous Chincoteague oysters have not been harvested for nearly a century. Instead, Chesapeake Bay oysters are trucked to Chincoteague Bay, ferried one mile offshore, and dumped into the brine. What is dredged up two months later may not be original, but it makes a lot of people happy, including the oystermen of Smith Island.

It is doubtful you will ever sample a Chincoteague oyster stew, pie, or puff. An oyster that salty is simply too tasty and lucrative on the half shell for it to be sacrificed to the cooking pot. Instead, be satisfied with Bay oysters for your recipes, adding salt for the ocean tang. Mrs. Kitching recommends "salting to locality"; that is, adding more salt to the bland, fresher water oysters of the Upper Bay and less salt to the brinier Lower Bay oysters.

Buy only standard oysters, the smallest and least expensive size, for your recipes. They are younger and more tender than selects and extra-selects. Oysters need never be washed in water. Packaged fresh oysters have been thoroughly cleaned in the shucking house. If you shuck your own, wash and scrub the shells in water beforehand. Let them sit in their liquor after being shucked so that the grit will settle to the bottom. Then feel through the lacy gill folds while in the liquor to loosen additional particles of grit.

If you must keep your oysters for a while before cooking, refrigerate and use within seven to ten days. Mrs. Kitching does not freeze fresh oysters because they lose their flavor. When you refrigerate oysters in the shell, be sure all of them are alive before using. An open shell should close immediately upon being touched. The shell is open in the refrigerator because the oyster, still alert to the rhythms of its home environment, is trying to feed on the flood tide. Keep shell oysters in the refrigerator, on ice or outside providing the temperature stays around thirty-five degrees Fahrenheit. Store no longer than three weeks.

Steamed Oysters Topped with Cheese

Oysters in the shell, as many as desired
Mozzarella cheese 1 tablespoon per oyster, grated

Wash and scrub shell oysters in water. Place on a heavy baking sheet, and bake in a 400 degree oven for about five minutes or until shells open. Sever the muscle and remove the top shell. Sprinkle the oyster on the half shell with the grated cheese and eat when melted.

Raw Box

1 dozen medium sized oysters in the shell
1/2 cup vinegar
salt and pepper to taste
soda crackers

Combine vinegar, salt, and pepper. Scrub oyster shells, then shuck. Dip individual oysters into vinegar and eat with crackers.

Oyster Pie

1 9 inch pie crust and cover
1 pint standard oysters with liquor
1 small onion, diced
1/2 cup evaporated milk
1/2 cup water
salt and pepper to taste

Combine oysters in their liquor with onion, milk, water, salt, and pepper. Pour into pie shell, cover with pastry top, and bake at 350 degrees for one hour or until top crust is browned.

Barbecued Oysters

1	pint standard oysters, drained
1/2	pound bacon
1	cup barbecue sauce (recipe to follow)
1/2	cup grated mozzarella cheese, optional

Cut each strip of bacon into thirds. Wrap individual oysters in the bacon strips and secure with toothpicks. Marinate in barbecue sauce for 45 minutes. Top with cheese, if desired. Place on a cookie sheet and broil for 10 - 12 minutes at 450 degrees. Yield about 30 to 40.

Barbecue Sauce

1/4	cup ketchup
1/4	cup water
2	tablespoons vinegar
2	tablespoons sugar
1	tablespoon dry mustard
1	tablespoon Worcestershire Sauce
	dash chili powder

Combine all ingredients in a medium size bowl. Stir until blended.

Oyster Puffs

1	pint standard oysters, drained
3/4	cup self-rising flour or pancake mix
1	teaspoon baking powder
	salt and pepper to taste
1/2	cup evaporated milk
	vegetable oil, enough to fill frying pan 1 - 1 1/2 inch deep

Combine flour, baking powder, salt, and pepper. Stir milk into mixture to make a batter. Add oysters without liquor to the batter and coat thoroughly. Remove individual oysters with a fork and drop into hot oil in frying pan. (The oil is ready when a drop of water spatters upon contact with it.) Oysters will puff a few seconds after hitting the hot oil. Fry the puffs on both sides until golden. Yield: 30 to 40.

Fried Oysters

1	pint standard oysters, drained
3/4	cup flour
1	teaspoon baking powder
	salt and pepper to taste
1	cup evaporated milk
	vegetable oil, enough to fill a frying pan 1/4 inch deep

Combine flour, baking powder, salt, and pepper. Stir milk into mixture to make a thin batter. Add the oysters without liquor to the batter and stir. Heat the oil in the frying pan. When oil is hot, spoon oysters individually with generous amount of the batter into the hot oil. Make each patty about the size of a half dollar. Fry the oysters on both sides until golden. Yield: 30 to 40.

Scalloped Oysters

1	pint standard oysters with liquor
1	package (or 40) unsalted soda crackers
	salt and pepper to taste
3	tablespoons butter
1	small onion, grated, optional
1/2 - 1	cup evaporated milk or heavy cream

Grease 1 1/2-quart casserole with one tablespoon of the butter. Crumble 3/4 package (or 30) of crackers and spread evenly on the bottom of casserole. Place oysters side by side on top of crackers. Salt and pepper to taste. Add a small amount of grated onion, if desired. Crumble remaining crackers and cover oyster layer. Dab top cracker layer with pieces of remaining two tablespoons of butter. Pour oyster liquor into a one-cup measure and add evaporated milk or cream until a full cup is reached. Pour the liquid uniformly over the oysters. Bake at 350 degrees for 35 to 40 minutes or until golden.

Breaded Baked Oysters

1	pint standard oysters, drained
1	egg
	salt and pepper to taste
1/2	cup milk
1/2	package (or 20) unsalted soda crackers
1/4	cup butter
1/4	pound medium sharp cheese, optional

Beat the egg and add milk, salt and pepper. Crumble the crackers, preferably in a blender, to a very fine consistency. Dip each oyster into egg mixture, then dredge in cracker meal. Melt butter and pour into 1 1/2-quart casserole. Place the breaded oysters in the casserole dish. Grate cheese over top and bake at 400 degrees for 10 to 15 minutes.

CHAPTER FOUR

Spring

Spring is coming. Oyster yields are lean. Watermen tarry longer in the general stores. Talk has turned to the next season. As early as March 1, islanders are anticipating the change, reading signs no meteorologist would dare predict with: fig trees are budding; marsh hawks have returned; and the wind is coming around to the south. It may be "rainin' a flood 'n blowin' a gale" beyond the door, but winter, so the old heads say, is over.

Prognostications aside, the most telling sign of spring is the last day of oystering. That date, usually March 31, initiates a refreshing lull in the rhythm of island life. Watermen sleep until dawn. Workboats are pulled up and overhauled. Women spade gardens and turn houses inside out in a fit of cleaning. So synchronized are the islanders's schedules with nature's timetable that the only respite they have is the hiatus between oystering and crabbing. Not until the crabs start stirring, migrating across the Maryland line in late April, will the men resume their business of "following the water."

Happily, nature brooks no favorites when awarding her holiday. The whole world around Smith Island goes on vacation at once. The sky, the wind, and the marsh scintillate in the warming sunlight. Wildlife is more visible and more beautiful as its numbers primp for the mating season. Flocks of cranes, egrets, herons, and ibises daily replace departing ducks and geese. North of Ewell, their rookeries fill entire islands. "Cherry Tree", a seven hundred by one hundred-yard insular jungle, hosts an estimated two thousand nesting birds including rare-to-Maryland roseate spoonbills and several species never before reported in the United States. Although every islander owns the means to take you to these isolated spots, few will oblige. "Too much to do to go gallavantin'," was the chastening response to an inquiry about skiff transportation. "There was one girl wanted me to take her and leave her," the man added. "That's where she'd be found, too."

No one stays in the marshes any longer than he has to. Swarms of green flies, sheep flies, mosquitoes, and gnats approach man-eating proportions after spring's first hot spell. The watermen are inured to the harassment. Their indifference is most evident when they are being bitten. Five, ten, fifteen seconds will pass before the brawny hand strikes out at an ensconced "greenhead." " 'Used to 'em," is all they say. One tormented visitor asked a retired water-man how he suffered all the flies. "I don't," came the reply. "I kill 'em. But I leave some for the next person."

Tolerance was not always so easy. Some years ago residents voted to spray their villages with insecticides. The subsequent disappearance of purple martins from backyard birdhouses proved too great a price to pay for comfort. The spraying stopped, and the purple martins eventually returned. Similarly, when the eelgrass on the crab bottoms started dying in great swaths for no apparent reason, folks became alarmed. Eelgrass is the primary cover for Atlantic blue crabs in their vulnerable soft shell stage. Though science has drawn no conclusions, a number of islanders are urging the investigation of pesticide runoff from mainland farms.

Smith Islanders are finely tuned to their natural environment. They must be. Their livelihoods, even their lives, depend upon acute powers of observation. They may joke about their precarious lot in life: "If you're lookin' for somethin' in a fog an' when you get there an' it ain't there—damn—if you ain't lost." They may protest the eternal vagaries of nature: "Cain't trust a radio forecast—too many weather patterns on the Bay. What's slick ca'm here could be blowin' you out of the water ten miles away." And often, they resort to the time-tested lore of elders: "That mornin' sun looks like someone's settin' on her, you're gonna have it ca'm. If she comes up perfectly round, not too red, it'll be pretty apt to blow." But to a man, they will never fail to keep an eye on the horizon, a nose to windward, and a prayer in their hearts.

Religion is as natural to these people as breathing. Living with so much uncertainty and danger, their religion, Methodism, im-parts the strength of faith. That faith manifests itself in whole-hearted worship. For six days a week they toil; then, on "the Lord's Day" they relax with class meeting, morning service, Sunday school, and evening service. They enjoy their religion. They even yarn about it.

> This man, Dave, was real religious. When the preach-er'd be preachin', he'd get up 'n holler, "Amen!," all the

100

time. Whenever that preacher'd make a good point, Dave'd say, "Amen! AMEN!"

His wife now, she was embarassed, seein' him jumpin' up in church. She noticed other people's husbands weren't a'doin' it. So she said, "If you won't say Amen 'n jump up in church no more, I'll buy you a brand new suit o' oilskins."

The next Sunday they went to church. The preacher come in 'n he was preachin' fire 'n lightnin'. Dave was holdin' hisself back. Restrainin' hisself. When all of a sudden that preacher—oh—he come in with the greatest point of all. Dave jumped up 'n hollered, "OILSKINS OR NO OILSKINS! AMEN!"

There is no separation, on Smith Island, between church and state. The church runs the dental clinic, hires the nurse, pays for street lights, organizes recreational functions, and maintains order. The island is run by a theocracy of the Methodist Church, and it is successful. For over three hundred years, no one has locked a door. After a waterman's life savings were stolen from his home during the Freeze of '77, folks were nonplused. But, they did not change. Said one man, "I guess we'll get to wonderin' if someone turns up with a new oyster boat." The theft was, after all, the only crime anyone could remember.

Smith Island watermen have always lived outside the law. Their occupation and their communities derive from, what they consider, their God-given right to nature's providence. It is impossible to tell them what to do: they fear no one; and they usually know more about their domain than the experts. That is why it took a waterman like themselves to show them the light.

In the early nineteenth century, Joshua Thomas brought to the islands of the lower Chesapeake a religious philosophy and fervor that converted thousands. His style was persuasive. When the British occupied Tangier Island prior to their invasion of Baltimore in 1814, this "Parson of the Islands" exhorted the regiments. ". . . it was given me from the Almighty that they could not take Baltimore." Baltimore was not taken, and the vanquished soldiers later reported that the Parson ". . . seemed to be standing right before us still warning us against our attempt."

Legend has it that an English soldier, who died on board ship after the battle, was buried on Smith Island. On request, the British Navy recently examined its ships' logs of the period for notation of such an occurrence. None was found. As strong as oral tradition is on the island, one cannot stand by the unmarked grave at Pitchcroft without wondering if the British are in error.

On a cool spring evening with the sun orange over the marshes, Pitchcroft is an experience in insular remoteness. The old house by the gravesite is vacant, and the only creatures about are cats, furtive remnants of the previous summer's glut. Pitchcroft was a meadow once, but now waves wash the edge of the lawn. Two hundred years ago goats and cattle grazed on the site, surmises Captain William Somers, and the farm may have produced pitch for ships' hulls. The biggest tree on the island grows there, darkly guarding an old cemetery. Its roots probe far beneath the island's six foot deep, saline water table and hold together a good bit of Ewell. Only neighborhood artesian wells, drilled a thousand feet down to spring water under the Bay bottom, go deeper. The silence on Pitchcroft is ephemeral, however. As soon as yonder village supper hour concludes, pandemonium ensues.

At 6 P.M., the teenaged contingent hits the road. Radios blare, and engines roar. Mufflers in terminal stages of corrosion reverberate from Ewell to Rhodes Point like the mating call of machine guns. Three miles of lane, only a tad wider than outstretched arms, accommodate trucks, cars, scooters and motorcycles. Few vehicles bear tags, and fewer remain intact. The attrition rate is high, and all eventually land in the dump on the middle of the island. In 1970, the Army Corps of Engineers arranged to dispose of all abandoned cars cluttering backyards and roadsides. "They took 'em alroight," said one resident. "No further than the middle of the island."

The teenagers are not complaining. The dump is one place everyone else avoids. There are no theaters, bars, or liquor stores on Smith Island, and only one recreational hall. School is a one room primary school in Tylerton, or the primary and junior high in Ewell. Not every grade has children, and one teacher instructs several grades. High school is on the mainland. Since 1974, a school boat has been available for daily rather than weekly crossings. The 7:30 A.M. to 4:30 P.M. trek is futile to some students. "You cain't stay after school for sports or extracurricular activities and they [mainlanders] think we live in caves and don't pay taxes." Of nine Smith Islanders in the Crisfield High School Class of 1980, six remain on the island (three as watermen), one joined the army, and two go to college.

The biggest problem facing Smith Island is not the departure of its young people. The waterman's life will always appeal to upcoming generations if the seafood harvest is lucrative. What troubles

102

Smith Islanders is more serious. In fifty to one hundred years, if preventive measures are not taken, Smith Island will be gone. The Chesapeake Bay is eroding the island at an average rate of eight shore feet a year. By 1990, according to an Army Corps of Engineers report, the western edge of marsh protecting the island from open bay will be washed away. By the twenty-first century, high tide will inundate all but the highest ground.

The Chesapeake Bay has a history of swallowing its islands. Within the twentieth century, Sharp's and Sprye have disappeared. Watts is almost gone. The last inhabitant of three hundred on Holland's Island bailed out in 1922. Now, Smith Island's life hangs in the balance. The question is: Can the exorbitant cost of shoring up the island be justified by the benefit to comparatively few people? The alternative, however, is the loss of Maryland's last island community and the end of three centuries of Chesapeake Bay tradition.

Since the beginning of America, Smith Islanders have made their own way in the world. It is time they got a little help.

SUNDRY KITCHING FAVORITES

DESSERTS

Peach Pie

1	9-inch unbaked pie shell
4	cups peeled, sliced peaches
1	cup sugar
1	egg, well beaten
1	cup milk
2	tablespoons cornstarch
1/2	teaspoon cinnamon

Pour half the sugar over the sliced peaches and set aside. In a bowl, combine milk and cornstarch. Stir to dissolve cornstarch. Add beaten egg and remaining sugar. Pour mixture over peaches. Sprinkle cinnamon inside unbaked pie shell. Pour peach filling into pie shell and bake at 350 degrees for 45 minutes to one hour.

Hot Milk Cake

1	cup milk
1/2	cup butter
2	cups flour, sifted
2	teaspoons baking powder
1	teaspoon salt
4	eggs
2	cups sugar
1	teaspoon vanilla

In a saucepan, heat the milk and butter until butter is melted. Do not scald. On a plate, sift together flour, baking powder, and salt. In a separate mixing bowl, beat eggs until light and fluffy. Slowly add sugar to eggs until sugar is well dissolved. Add one third of the dry, sifted ingredients to the egg mixture; then add one third of the hot milk (which has been allowed to cool during subsequent preparations). Beat well. Continue alternating thirds of wet and dry ingredients to egg mixture until they are used up. Beat the batter between thirds until smooth and without air bubbles. Pour into greased 10-inch tube pan and bake at 350 degrees for 30 minutes.

Jewish Apple Cake

5	large, unpeeled apples
	cinnamon sugar in a ratio of 2 teaspoons cinnamon to 1 tablespoon sugar
4	eggs
2 1/4	cups sugar
1	cup vegetable oil
3	cups flour
3	teaspoons baking powder
1/2	teaspoon salt
1/2	cup orange juice
1 1/4	teaspoons vanilla

Core and slice apples. Put in a bowl and sprinkle with cinnamon sugar. Beat eggs and gradually add sugar. Add vegetable oil. Sift together dry ingredients and mix into batter. Add orange juice and vanilla. Grease a tube pan, then dust with flour. Pour 1/3 of batter into pan. Layer with 1/3 of apples. Repeat for 2 more layers. Bake at 350 degrees for 1 1/2 hours.

Pineapple Custard Pie

1	9-inch baked pie shell
1	cup crushed pineapple
1	cup sugar
1	cup evaporated milk
	pinch salt
2	eggs, separated
2	tablespoons flour
1/4	cup water
1	teaspoon vanilla
1/2	tablespoon butter

In a saucepan, combine pineapple, sugar, milk, and salt. Beat egg yolks and add to saucepan. Dissolve flour in water and add to saucepan. Cook over medium heat, stirring constantly until thickened. Remove from heat and add vanilla and butter. Pour into pie shell. Top with meringue (recipe on page 108) and bake at 350 degrees just until meringue is golden brown, about 10 minutes.

Fig Cake

1 1/2	cups sugar
1	cup vegetable oil
3	eggs
2	cups flour
1	teaspoon baking soda
1	teaspoon cinnamon
1	teaspoon nutmeg
1	teaspoon allspice
1	teaspoon salt
1/2	cup buttermilk
1	teaspoon vanilla
1	cup fig preserves
1	cup chopped nuts

Blend together sugar, oil, and eggs. On a plate, sift together the dry ingredients. Add sifted, dry ingredients in thirds to egg mixture, alternating with thirds of buttermilk. Add vanilla and mix until smooth. Fold in figs and nuts. Pour into greased tube pan or 2 greased loaf pans. Bake at 350 degrees for one hour.

Fig Cake Icing

1	cup sugar
1/2	cup buttermilk
1/4	cup butter
1	teaspoon baking soda
1	tablespoon corn syrup
1	teaspoon vanilla

Combine all ingredients except vanilla. Cook in saucepan slowly to the soft ball stage (until a small quantity dropped into ice water forms a ball which does not disintegrate). Remove from heat, add vanilla and beat until blended. Pour over cooled cake.

Poor Man's Cake

1	15-ounce box raisins
3	cups water
2	cups sugar
3/4	cups vegetable shortening
1	teaspoon cinnamon
1	teaspoon allspice
1	teaspoon nutmeg
1	teaspoon ginger
1	teaspoon salt
3	cups flour
1	cup applesauce
1	teaspoon baking soda
1	cup chopped nuts
1	cup fig preserves

Immerse raisins in 2 cups water. Cook for 20 minutes until soft, then add sugar and shortening while hot. Let cool. Pour into mixing bowl. Sift dry ingredients and mix into raisins. Stir in applesauce. Dissolve baking soda in one cup water and add to cake batter. Blend well. Fold in nuts and figs. Pour into greased bundt pan. Bake at 350 degrees for 55 minutes.

Cinnamon Peach Cake

1	cup sugar
3/4	cup butter
2	teaspoons vegetable shortening
2 1/2	cups flour
1/2	teaspoon salt
3	teaspoons baking powder
1	cup milk
2	cups canned peaches, drained or 2 cups sliced fresh peaches with 1/4 cup sugar mixed in cinnamon sugar in a ratio of 2 teaspoons cinnamon to 1 tablespoon sugar

Cream together sugar, 1/4 cup butter, and shortening. On a plate, sift together dry ingredients. Add sifted, dry ingredients in thirds to butter mixture alternating with thirds of milk. Beat batter smooth between thirds. Add vanilla and blend. Pour batter into two greased 9-inch cake pans or one 9 × 13-inch pan. Spread peaches on top and sprinkle with cinnamon sugar. Bake at 350 degrees for 30 minutes. When baked, sprinkle again with cinnamon sugar and pour 1/2 cup melted butter over top.

Meringue

2	egg whites
4	teaspoons sugar
	pinch salt
	dash cream of tartar

Beat egg whites until stiff. Add sugar slowly beating all the while. Add salt and cream of tartar. (A good rule of thumb in making meringue is to allow 2 teaspoons of sugar for each egg white used.)

Lemon Fluff

1	3-ounce package lemon jello
1	cup water
1	13-ounce can evaporated milk
1	cup powdered sugar
2	tablespoons lemon juice
	vanilla wafers

Chill evaporated milk. Dissolve jello in one cup water and let gel slightly. Whip evaporated milk (after chilling) until stiff. To milk, add sugar, lemon juice, and jello. Line shallow baking dish with vanilla wafers. Pour jello mixture over top. Crumble wafers on top and refrigerate until firm.

Applesauce Pie

2	unbaked 9-inch pie crusts
1	16 1/2-ounce container of applesauce or 1 pint homemade applesauce
1	cup sugar
4	eggs, separated
1/2	cup butter
2	tablespoons cornstarch
1	teaspoon vanilla or lemon flavoring or
1/2	teaspoon cinnamon
2	cups evaporated milk
1/2	cup whole milk

Put applesauce in a bowl. Add sugar, egg yolks, butter, cornstarch, and your choice of a flavoring and mix until smooth. Add evaporated milk. In separate bowl, beat egg whites until stiff. Fold egg whites into applesauce mixture. Stir whole milk into mixture very slowly. Pour into two pie shells. Bake at 400 degrees for 15 minutes; then 350 degrees for 25 minutes.

Pecan Dreams

1 3/4	cups pecans, chopped
1	cup butter
2	tablespoons powdered sugar plus additional powdered sugar to roll cookies in
2	teaspoons water
2	teaspoons vanilla
2	cups flour

Cream butter and sugar. Add water and vanilla. Add flour and pecans and beat until mixture is uniform. Form small balls by rolling pieces in hands. Bake at 300 degrees for 20 minutes. When cookies cool enough to handle, roll each one in powdered sugar. Yield: 50 cookies.

Smith Island Ten-Layer Cake

2	cups sugar
2	sticks unsalted butter, cut into chunks
5	eggs
3	cups flour
1/4	teaspoon salt
1	heaping teaspoon baking powder
1	cup evaporated milk
2	teaspoons vanilla
1/2	cup water

Cream together sugar and butter. Add eggs one at a time and beat until smooth. Sift together flour, salt, and baking powder. Mix into egg mixture one cup at a time. With mixer running, slowly pour in the evaporated milk, then the vanilla and water. Mix just until uniform.

Put three serving spoonfuls of batter in each of ten 9-inch lightly greased pans, using the back of the spoon to spread evenly. Bake three layers at a time on the middle rack of the oven at 350 degrees for 8 minutes. A layer is done when you hold it near your ear and you don't hear it sizzle.

Start making the icing when the first layers go in the oven. Put the cake together as the layers are finished. Let the layers cool a couple of minutes in the pans. Run a spatula around the edge of the pan and ease the layer out of the pan. Don't worry if it tears; no one will notice when the cake is finished. Use two or three serving spoonfuls of icing between each layer. Cover the top and sides of the cake with the rest of the icing. Push icing that runs onto the plate back onto the cake.

Chocolate Icing for Ten-Layer Cake

2	cups sugar
1	cup evaporated milk
5	ounces unsweetened chocolate
1	stick unsalted butter
1/2 to 1 teaspoon vanilla	

Put sugar and evaporated milk in a medium pan. Cook and stir over medium-low heat until warm. Add chocolate and cook to melt. Add butter and melt. Cook over medium heat at a slow boil for 10 to 15 minutes. Stir occasionally. Add vanilla. Icing will be thin, but thickens as it cools.

Blackberry Cobbler

1	quart blackberries
1	cup sugar
2	tablespoons cornstarch
3/4	cup water
1	teaspoon ground cinnamon
1	tablespoon butter
1	cup flour, sifted
1 1/2	teaspoon baking powder
1/2	teaspoon salt
1/3	cup milk
3	tablespoons vegetable oil

Combine sugar, cornstarch, water, and cinnamon over medium heat. Stir constantly and allow to boil for one minute. Add butter and allow to melt. Add blackberries. In a separate bowl, mix together milk, oil, and sifted dry ingredients to form dough. Pour one half of blackberry mixture into 1 1/2-quart baking dish. Drop spoonfuls of dough on top of blackberry mixture until dough is used up. Pour rest of blackberry mixture over top. Bake at 425 degrees for 25 minutes.

Banana Nut Bread

3	cups mashed bananas
1/2	cup butter
1 1/2	cups sugar
2	eggs, separated
1	teaspoon vanilla
2	cups flour
1/2	teaspoon salt
1	teaspoon baking powder
4	tablespoons buttermilk
1/2	cup chopped walnuts

Cream together butter and sugar. Add egg yolks and beat well. Add mashed bananas and vanilla. Mix well. Sift together flour, salt, and baking powder and add to banana mixture alternating with portions of buttermilk until batter is smooth. Add nuts. In separate bowl, beat egg whites until stiff. Fold into banana batter. Pour into two greased loaf pans and bake at 350 degrees for 40 to 45 minutes.

Peanut Butter Cookies

1	cup peanut butter
1	cup vegetable shortening
1	cup sugar
2	eggs, beaten
1	tablespoon milk
2	cups flour
1/2	teaspoon salt
1/2	teaspoon baking soda

Cream together shortening and sugar. Beat in eggs. Add peanut butter and milk, and blend well. Sift dry ingredients together and add slowly, beating all the while, to the cookie batter. With a teaspoon form one inch balls and place on cookie sheet. Bake at 325 degrees for 15 to 20 minutes. Yield: 30 cookies.

Candy Cookies

3	cups rolled oats
2 1/2	cups sugar
2	tablespoons cocoa
1/2	cup milk
1	teaspoon vanilla
1/2	cup butter

Combine sugar, cocoa, milk, and vanilla in saucepan. Boil for 2 minutes. Remove from heat. Add butter. When melted, stir in rolled oats. With teaspoon, drop one inch balls onto wax paper. Let cool. Yield: 30 cookies.

SALADS

Fresh Peach Salad

9	fresh peaches, peeled and sliced
1/4	cup sugar
1	tablespoon mayonnaise
1	cup sour cream

Mix together sugar, mayonnaise, and sour cream. Pour over peaches. Chill. Serve on bed of lettuce.

Bean Salad

1	15 1/2-ounce can French cut green beans
1	15 1/2-ounce can yellow beans
1	15 1/2-ounce can kidney beans
1	16-ounce can lima beans, optional
1/2	cup diced celery
1	2-ounce jar pimento
1	large red onion, sliced thin and separated into rings
3/4	cup vinegar
3/4	cup sugar
1/4	cup water
1/3	cup vegetable oil
1/2	teaspoon salt

Drain all beans, then rinse in colander with cold water and allow to drain. Add celery, drained chopped pimento and onion to beans. Combine vinegar, sugar, water, oil, and salt to beans and lightly toss. Refrigerate for at least two hours and serve.

Strawberry Nut Gelatin Salad

1	3-ounce package strawberry jello
1	cup boiling water
2	10-ounce packages frozen strawberries
1	cup chopped nuts
1	1 pound 4-ounce can crushed pineapple, drained
2	bananas
1	pint sour cream

Combine jello and hot water, and stir until jello is dissolved. Fold in thawed strawberries, nuts, pineapple, bananas, and sour cream. Chill in a mold until firm.

Fresh Cranberry Salad

1	pound fresh cranberries, washed
3	unpeeled oranges, sliced
4	unpeeled apples, sliced and cored
2	cups sugar

In a blender, grind cranberries, apples and oranges to a coarse consistency. Add sugar. Mix well and chill.

Salad Dressing

1	egg, beaten
3	tablespoons sugar
1	tablespoon flour
2	tablespoons water
1	teaspoon salt
1	tablespoon dry mustard
3	tablespoons vinegar
1	cup evaporated milk

Dissolve flour in water. Add rest of ingredients and cook over direct heat until thickened. Cool.

Ham Potato Salad Loaf

6	ounces chopped ham
1	envelope gelatin
1/2	cup water
1	cup mayonnaise
1	teaspoon salt
1	teaspoon minced onion
1/4	cup parsley
1/4	teaspoon green and/or red pepper
4	stalks celery, diced
4	cups cooked diced potatoes

Line a 9 × 5-inch loaf pan with foil extending over sides. Line bottom and sides with ham. Dissolve gelatin in water over hot water in double boiler. Add remaining ingredients. Stir gently to blend. Pack mixture into pan and chill until firm. Turn out on to a cold platter. Garnish with lettuce and tomatoes.

Banana Pepper Relish

1	dozen sweet peppers
2	dozen banana peppers
3	hot peppers
7	medium yellow onions
3	cups vinegar
2	cups sugar
2	tablespoons dry mustard
2	tablespoons salt

Chop peppers and onions to a fine, uniform consistency. In large saucepan, combine remaining ingredients and stir over heat to dissolve sugar. Add peppers and onions. Bring to a boil and continue to boil for 30 minutes. Pack in sterilized jars.

Pepper Relish

12	green peppers
12	red peppers
12	large yellow onions
2	cups sugar
1	quart vinegar

Chop peppers and onions to a fine, uniform consistency. In large saucepan, combine vinegar and sugar, and stir over medium heat until sugar is dissolved. Add chopped peppers and onions. Bring to a boil and continue boiling for 10 minutes. Put into sterilized jars and seal.

Pickled Pears

12-15	small pears, peeled
1	cup sugar
1	cup vinegar
1/2	box cloves (1 1/8-ounce box), tied in small cheesecloth bag

Immerse bag of cloves in vinegar. Add sugar and bring to a boil. Add pears and cook until tender. Remove bag of cloves. Put pears with syrup in sterilized jars. Seal and store.

Pickled Watermelon Rind

1	cup cubed watermelon rind
1	teaspoon salt
1	cup sugar
1	cup vinegar
2	tablespoons whole cloves

Peel hard skin from watermelon rind. Cube the rind. Place in a bowl, cover with water and salt, and store overnight in refrigerator. Drain salt water. Combine sugar, vinegar, and cloves tied in cheesecloth bag. Bring to a boil and add rind. Boil until rind is tender. Remove bag of cloves. Put rind with syrup into sterilized jars. Seal and store.

Bread and Butter Pickles

1	gallon sliced cucumbers
4	large white onions, sliced
1/2	cup salt
5	cups sugar
5	cups vinegar
1 1/2	teaspoons cloves
1 1/2	teaspoons tumeric
2	tablespoons mustard seed
2	tablespoons celery seed

Combine sliced cucumbers, onions, and salt in a bowl. Cover with water and set aside for 3 hours. Combine remaining ingredients in saucepan. Bring to a boil. Drain water from cucumbers and onions and add them to boiling pickling juice. Cook everything for 20 minutes, then pour into sterilized jars. Seal and store.

Pomegranate Jelly

10-15	ripe pomegranates
8	cups sugar
1	6-ounce bottle fruit pectin

Prepare pomegranates by cutting each one in half. Ream each half on an orange juice squeezer. Place pulp and seeds in cheesecloth and squeeze out juice. Measure 4 cups of pomegranate juice into a large saucepan. Add sugar and fruit pectin and bring to a full boil. Boil for one minute, stirring constantly. Remove from heat, skim off foam, and quickly pour into jelly glasses. Cover with 1/8-inch paraffin wax and store.

Fig Preserves

1	quart figs
2	cups sugar
1/2	lemon, sliced

Peel skins off figs and pour sugar over top. Cook over low heat until mushy. Add sliced lemon. Cook until syrup thickens. Skim off foam while cooking. Pour figs into sterilized jars, topping with syrup. Seal and store.

MISCELLANEOUS

Chicken Casserole

1	2-3 pound frying chicken, cut up
1	10 3/4-ounce can cream of chicken soup
1	10 3/4-ounce can cream of celery soup
1	10 3/4-ounce can cream of mushroom soup
1	13-ounce can evaporated milk
1	envelope onion soup mix (2 3/4-ounce package)
1	cup rice

Mix together soups and evaporated milk. Add half the mixture to deep 2-quart casserole. Sprinkle rice over soup, then add rest of soup. Place chicken pieces in a layer over soup and sprinkle onion soup mixture on top. Cover and bake at 350 degrees for 1 3/4 hours.

Gringo Cabbage

1	medium sized head of cabbage
1	cup buttered bread crumbs
1	cup grated American cheese
1	teaspoon salt
1/2	cup butter
1/4	teaspoon cayenne pepper
3	teaspoons flour
1 1/2	cups milk
	boiling water

Chop cabbage coarsely into large saucepan and add 1/2 teaspoon salt. Cover with boiling water. Put over heat and boil for 7 minutes. Drain the water. Place half the cabbage in a shallow rectangular baking dish. Melt butter in saucepan. Add flour, rest of salt, and pepper. Stir to a paste. Slowly add milk and stir constantly until a smooth white sauce results. Pour half of white sauce over cabbage in baking dish. Sprinkle with half the cheese and half the bread crumbs. Layer with remaining cabbage, cheese, and bread crumbs. Pour remaining white sauce over top. Bake at 350 degrees for 30 minutes.

Homemade Scrapple

2	pounds pork liver
1	pounds lean salt pork
1 1/2	cups flour
1 1/2	cups cornmeal
1	teaspoon sage

Cut up meat in cubes. Add to 1 1/2 quarts of water. Cook meat until tender. Drain and save liquid. Mash meat and add liquid. Sift together dry ingredients and add to mashed meat and liquid as it simmers on stove. Stir constantly to keep from sticking. Pour into baking dish and let stand until gelled. Eat hot, or store in refrigerator to slice and fry later.

Fried Tomatoes

4	tomatoes
3	tablespoons butter
1/3	cup milk
1/2	cup flour
	salt and pepper to taste
2	tablespoons brown sugar

Cut tomatoes into 1/2-inch thick slices. Dredge in flour, salt, and pepper. Melt 2 tablespoons of butter in frying pan. When melted, fry tomatoes until browned on both sides. Remove tomatoes and add rest of butter to pan drippings, plus milk and one tablespoon of the leftover flour. Stir to a sauce. Pour over tomatoes, and sprinkle brown sugar on top.

Popovers

1	cup sifted flour
2	eggs, beaten
1	cup milk
1/4	teaspoon salt
1	medium diced onion, optional

Combine all ingredients. Beat at high speed for 3 minutes. Pour in greased muffin tin, filling each well half full. Bake at 450 degrees for 15 minutes, then reduce heat to 350 degrees and bake for 15 more minutes. Do not open oven door or popovers will fall.

Photographs

The photographs in *Mrs. Kitching's Smith Island Cookbook* were taken especially for the book. For those readers who are curious as to where particular photographs were taken, or of whom, here are some identifications. Pictures on pages 4-5, 12, 31 (bottom), 44, 47, 94, and 119 are by Robert Grieser. All others were taken by Marilyn Martin.

Index